More Than a
Numbers Game

More Than a Numbers Game

A Brief History of Accounting

Thomas A. King

WILEY

John Wiley & Sons, Inc.

Published by John Wiley & Sons, Inc., Hoboken, New Jersey.
Published simultaneously in Canada.

For general information on our other products and services or for technical
support, please contact our Customer Care Department within the United
States at (800) 762-2974, outside the United States at (317) 572-3993 or
fax (317) 572-4002.

Wiley also publishes its books in a variety of electronic formats. Some content
that appears in print may not be available in electronic books. For more
information about Wiley products, visit our web site at www.wiley.com.

Library of Congress Cataloging-in-Publication Data:

King, Thomas A., 1960–
    More than a numbers game : a brief history of accounting / Thomas A. King.
        p.   cm.
    Includes bibliographical references and index.
    ISBN-13: 978-0-470-00873-7 (cloth)
    ISBN-10: 0-470-00873-3 (cloth)
        1. Accounting—United States—History.   2. Accounting—Standards—
    United States—History.   3. Accounting—Law and legislation—United
    States—History.   I. Title.   II. Series.
    HF5616.U5K53   2006
    657.0973—dc22
                                                                    2005037200

Printed in the United States of America.

10 9 8 7 6 5 4 3 2 1

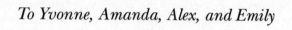

To Yvonne, Amanda, Alex, and Emily

CONTENTS

ABOUT THE COVER

The U.S. Postal Service and predecessor Post Office Department have released four thousand stamps to remember key people, places, and events in U.S. history. Stamps offer tiny windows into America's past. Six examples, presented from upper left to lower right on this book's cover, commemorate events discussed in this book.

Scott #1920. Issued September 21, 1987, to honor the 100th anniversary of the founding of the trade group that would become the American Institute of Certified Public Accountants. 22c; multicolored. Pen tip and ledger book, designed by Lou Nolan.

Scott #2361. Issued June 16, 1981, to observe the 100th anniversary of the founding of the Wharton School of Business. 18c; blue and black. Portrait of Joseph Wharton, designed by Rudolph de Harak.

Source: Scott Specialized Catalogue of US Stamps & Covers. Sidney, OH: Scott Publishing Company, 2000.

Scott #3184o. Issued May 28, 1998, as a pane of 15 stamps in the *Celebrate the Century* series' 1920s collection. Stock market crash of 1929. 32c; multicolored. Torn stock certificate, designed by Carl Herrman. Printed by Ashton-Potter (USA) Ltd.

Scott #922. Issued May 10, 1944, to celebrate the 75th anniversary of the completion of the first transcontinental railroad. 3c; violet. Based on *Golden Spike Ceremony*, painted by John McQuarrie.

Scott #1380. Issued September 22, 1969, to observe the 150th anniversary of the Dartmouth College case, where alumnus Daniel Webster argued before the Supreme Court that the government could not impair private contracts. 6c; green. Daniel Webster and Dartmouth Hall, designed by John R. Scotford Jr.

Scott #2630. Issued May 17, 1992, to honor the 200th anniversary of the founding of the market that became the New York Stock Exchange. 29c; green, red, and black. Stylized stock certificate, designed by Richard Sheaff. Printed by the Jeffries Bank Note Company for the American Bank Note Company.

PREFACE

The world suffers no shortage of accounting texts. The many I've read over the past 25 years have helped me audit, prepare, use, and explain corporate financial statements. Missing in this lettered journey has been a work that provides context for accounting's six divisive issues: inflation, volatility, intangibles, debt, options, and earnings. A brief history of accounting can fill this void.

Students and practitioners study textbooks designed to explain the how's of accounting. Readers consequently learn the mechanics of, say, calculating earnings per share without understanding that statement preparers and users often work at cross-purposes to cope with nonrecurring items and costs of equity-based compensation. This short book's contribution is to discuss the major why's of accounting practice.

More Than a Numbers Game was inspired by Arthur Levitt's landmark 1998 speech delivered at New York University. The Securities and Exchange Commission chairman described the too-little-challenged custom of earnings management and presaged the breakdown in U.S. corporate accounting three years later. Somehow, over a hundred-year period, accounting morphed from a tool used by American railroad managers to communicate with absent British investors into an enabler of corporate fraud. How this happened makes for a good story.

This book is not another description of accounting scandals but rather a history of ideas. Each chapter covers a controversial topic that emerged over the past century. Historical background and discussion of people involved give relevance to these concepts. I show how economics, finance, law, and business custom contributed to accounting's development. Use of anecdote, example, and light humor make *More Than a Numbers Game* easy to read.

Thoughts presented come from a career spent working with accounting information. I have designed and used cost accounting systems in manufacturing and service settings, argued with tax and regulatory authorities, and participated in design of compensation systems. Experience has shown me how numbers on paper influence careers, projects, and business prospects.

My credentials include tours of duty in financial statement auditing (auditor at a Big Eight accounting firm), preparation (corporate controller of a Fortune 500 firm), use (general manager with profit and loss responsibility at a corporation plus board member of a nonprofit), and explanation (accounting teacher and investor relations officer). Perhaps most significantly, I witnessed a major audit failure.

Accounting viewed from these perspectives taught me that the so-called language of business is best understood as a collection of dialects. Most accounting books spend too much time on financial reporting. Consideration of the purposes and limitations of cost, tax, and regulatory accounting makes the field more understandable to the informed layperson.

The reader who sticks with the text will be rewarded with a thorough grounding in accounting's major issues. By the final chapter, he or she should be able to engage in accounting debate on almost any topic. Accounting can be both a vocation and an avocation. It's fun. Really.

➤

Book prefaces, where authors thank others, seemed vacuous until I tried to put thoughts to paper. This book would not have been possible without generous support offered by colleagues. Marion Brakefield endured endless requests to modify charts. John Burchard and Scott Gould tracked down arcane articles and cases. Jeff Basch, Don Chew, and Tom Forrester provided helpful comments to improve presentation. John Wiley & Sons' Stacey Farkas, Bill Falloon, Pamela van Giessen, and Laura Walsh coached me with patience as I learned about the world of publishing. Their copyeditors possess a deft touch.

Thanks also to my father, who encouraged an accounting career. I hated my first job but slowly learned to appreciate accounting's hidden beauty. My grandfather exposed me to the craft of history and taught there are only three ways to know something: you experience it directly, someone tells you, or you figure it out. He also pressed the importance of active voice, strong verbs, and few prepositions.

The Ohio Library and Information Network, which delivered volumes from Ohio's college and university book collections to our neighborhood public library branch, made research possible in light of concurrent work and family commitments. Finally, my superiors chose not to fire me as I devoted increasing amounts of company time to complete this effort, a further illustration of Michael Jensen's agency costs.

Opinions and conclusions expressed herein represent personal views. No practitioner, academic, or regulator will agree with all points made in subsequent pages. I took liberties condensing ideas and events to keep this work brief. Responsibility for resulting errors and omissions rests with me.

Chagrin Falls, Ohio
November 2005

1

DOUBLE-ENTRY

What advantage does he derive from the system of bookkeeping by double-entry! It is among the finest inventions of the human mind.

—Johann Wolfgang von Goethe,
Wilhelm Meister, 1824

On Sunday, April 8, 1984, the phone rang in my Hoboken apartment. A Big Eight audit manager, my boss' boss, shared in a raspy voice that we had an accounting crisis. *Accounting crisis?* Jumbo shrimp, gunboat diplomacy, gourmet pizza, and other snappy phrases came to mind. *Hey, let's book another entry.*

The manager had learned that a client had amassed a sizable bond position and sustained adverse interest rate changes. Financial statements recently filed with the Securities and Exchange Commission (SEC) made no mention of the investment or holding loss. One could argue that investors relying on the statements had been misled.

My first accounting professor, New York University's George Sorter, taught there was no such thing as an accounting mistake.

1

Estimates used to make timely journal entries create inevitable misstatement. Errors reverse as more information comes to light. Nothing goes wrong over the infinite life of the firm. Consistent with Dr. Sorter's teachings, the client's estimates were indeed corrected.

In addition, the firm reshuffled management, filed restated balances, weathered unflattering publicity, and sustained an SEC investigation. My employer paid a sizable malpractice settlement. And I learned that sterile accounting numbers could make all the difference in the world.

Two decades later, accounting scandal rocked American business. In just 12 months industry giants Enron, Global Crossing, and WorldCom imploded. Arthur Andersen & Company—their auditor, my old employer, and once the planet's mightiest certified public accountant (CPA) firm—ceased to exist. And Congress enacted the most sweeping securities law since the Great Depression. This spectacular meltdown sparked the following effort to chronicle American corporate accounting's history from the age of railroads to Sarbanes-Oxley legislation.

History tells a story, and no story can ever be complete. Historians must select from an infinite ocean of facts those few deemed significant. Selections become fact only by virtue of significance attached by authors.[1] These pages present my views of the significant facts that created one of the largest business scandals in U.S. history.

Corporate financial reporting emerged in nineteenth-century America when professionals applied quantitative methods to qualitative endeavors. Academics blended philosophy with mathematics to create symbolic logic. Alfred Marshall's *Principles of Economics* (1890) organized economic thought into a mathematical framework. Emile Durkheim's *Suicide* (1897) used statistics to describe individual behavior.[2] Sociologist Max Weber considered probability in causal explanation. Bookkeepers expressed transactions in dollar values.

Even though accounting serves proprietorships, partnerships, governments, and nonprofits, this book focuses on its use to U.S. corporations. Indefinite life, divisible ownership, and limited liability allowed corporations to dominate American business by the 1890s.[3] The corporate form was so effective in meeting society's commercial needs that venerable organizations like Lloyd's of London and Goldman Sachs chose to incorporate.[4]

Healthy corporations require protected property rights and liquid capital markets. An 1819 U.S. Supreme Court decision capped the government's power to interfere with private agreements. King George III had granted a 1769 charter to Dartmouth College, the last college formed before the American Revolution. Forty-six years later the New Hampshire legislature sought to turn the private college into a state university.

Alumnus Daniel Webster, a future congressman and secretary of state, successfully argued before Chief Justice John Marshall's Supreme Court that a state government had no right to modify or impair private contracts (U.S. Constitution, Article 1, Section 10, Clause 1). Webster's speech included the famous phrase that Dartmouth is a small college but there are those who love it. Marshall's decision affirmed that a private organization could go about its business without state interference.

In the 1790s a collection of merchants formed an exchange in lower Manhattan to trade government bonds. In March 1817, as the *Dartmouth* case was litigated, members drafted a constitution and named the group the New York Stock & Exchange Board. The organization later shortened its title to the New York Stock Exchange (NYSE). Synonymous with Wall Street, the NYSE evolved into the world's largest, most liquid stock market. Concentrating buyers and sellers provided efficient pricing and reduced ownership risk for equity securities.

Property rights and capital markets require a buffer from fraud. Numbers offer some protection. Quantitative discussion curbs management's ability to talk its way out of problems. An executive I knew controlled evasive subordinates by limiting their responses to yes, no, or a number. The U.S. government offered body counts as quantitative—and presumably more believable— evidence of progress in the Vietnam War. Computer makers spew statistics to suggest product superiority.

Accounting quantifies business communication. Financial accounting, the primary dialect, allows lenders and investors to assess the amount, timing, and certainty of a corporation's future cash flows. Creditors want to know if they'll get their money back; stock investors care about whether they can expect substantial future dividends. Financial accounting principles emerged to match revenues with expenses and determine a corporation's ability to pay interest or dividends from business activity in a given period.

With passage of U.S. income tax law, the federal government embraced accounting to measure taxable income. Tax accounting mutated into a system designed to determine when a taxpayer had the obligation and ability to pay tax bills. Companies then needed two sets of books.

Scale-sensitive enterprises like steel producers and car manufacturers developed enormous infrastructures to reduce unit costs. Massive, indirect costs could not be easily traced to individual products. Sophisticated companies developed allocation systems to ensure product prices recovered all resources consumed in production. Healthy manufacturing firms learned to keep a third set of books to refine cost accounting methods.

Some regulated companies then had to file reports demonstrating solvency or compliance with government rules. These lucky banks, insurers, utilities, and transportation firms required a fourth set of books to maintain business licenses. The language of business became the province of experts.

Accounting rules trace to bookkeeping practices. Master taught apprentice, and custom became precedent. Rules agreed upon in the United States coalesced into generally accepted accounting principles (GAAP). Not until the Great Depression did formal bodies document and propose revisions to GAAP. No one has successfully codified this amorphous rule set.

These grass roots lent financial reporting a practical bias. The organization to emerge as the leading force for accounting standards was the trade group representing independent auditors, the American Institute of Certified Public Accountants (AICPA). Ideas put forth by accounting educators and financial statement preparers carried less weight. Economists, who developed insight into the nature of capital markets, financial securities, and asset valuation, garnered little respect from the auditing profession and its clients.

What did resonate was summarization. Financial accounting proved brilliant at condensing myriad transactions into a single statistic, earnings per share (EPS), which could be shared among thousands of investors. The discipline emerged as the primary tool to communicate corporate position and performance to absentee investors and lenders. As the U.S. economy developed over the twentieth century, accounting matured to summarize increasingly complex transactions in simple terms.

Three events tainted this maturation. First, the need to collect income taxes and product costing information created dialects. No one stepped forward to harmonize record keeping practices among accounting's branches. The resulting lack of conformance, especially with tax accounting and the rise of pro forma earnings figures, validated a *Rashomon*-like belief that there was no negative consequence for reporting the same event in varied ways.

Second, the growth of services aggregating analyst earnings estimates led to a game where analysts and investors evaluated the quality of a firm's reported results by determining whether the company met or missed consensus earnings figures. Some management teams bowed to increasing pressure and reported a few additional pennies per share each accounting period to demonstrate mastery of business operations. Jimmying the books created bigger problems.

Finally, statement preparers ignored advancements in economics. University researchers developed tools to understand consequences of business transactions and reporting principles. Practitioners brushed off this work and developed misguided judgments about market behavior.

When certain firms' stock prices became overvalued in the 1990s, these three forces combined to create pathological fear among statement preparers of reporting volatile earnings and showing debt on the balance sheet. Resulting actions created a train wreck in 2002.

Accounting begins with the balance sheet, a two-sided chart presenting assets used to accomplish a firm's objectives together with claims outsiders hold on those assets. Double-entry bookkeeping, a term eluding satisfactory definition, developed to show that changes in assets influence claims on those assets. German philosopher Oswald Spengler wrote in *The Decline of the West* (1928) that the invention of double-entry bookkeeping was the decisive event in European economic history.

Double-entry bookkeeping does not affirm symmetry of the universe. The tool simply emerged as a practical way to keep track of an organization's resources. Entering transactions twice provides a check to ensure computational accuracy and allows managers to track asset ownership. Entrepreneurs use other means to track businesses. An accounting professor even demonstrated feasibility of a triple-entry bookkeeping system.

In a double-entry world, assets must equal the sum of liabilities and shareholders' equity. What we have equals what we owe plus what we own. Equity represents owners' interests in assets after satisfaction of all outside claims. In liquidation, a firm would sell assets, pay liabilities, and distribute any remainder to owners. Figure 1.1 illustrates this accounting identity.

Accounting principles turn on three concepts: recognition, valuation, and classification. Recognition determines when a tool or claim should be recorded on the books. Valuation ascribes a

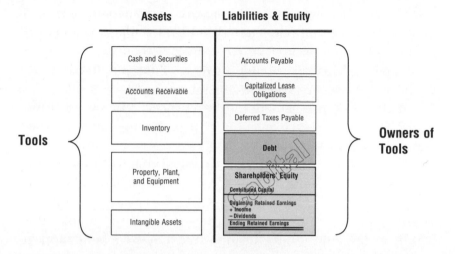

Figure 1.1   Balance Sheet Displays Claims on a Firm's Assets

dollar measurement to that tool or claim. Classification places the item somewhere in the geography of the balance sheet.

Assets generally appear on the balance sheet when a firm obtains rights to tools as a consequence of previous transactions. Accounting principles value most assets at historical cost with a downward revision, if appropriate, to cover deterioration or impairment. The cost convention arose from the need to place a monetary value on a future benefit with some degree of certainty.

Any veteran of garage sales recognizes the range of opinion associated with asset values. Accountants turned to historical cost, the cash used to buy the asset, as a solution. This sum represents what a willing buyer and seller agreed upon in an actual transaction. Auditors could verify this balance easily. Valuation of financial instruments, whose prices could be easily observed in security markets, began to be adjusted from acquisition cost to market quote.

Since 1894 the U.S. convention has been to classify assets in descending order of liquidity in order to make balance sheets more useful to creditors.[5] Assets that could not be easily converted into cash appeared further down the balance sheet's left-hand side. Suppliers, banks, and bondholders looked for liquid assets as potential collateral to secure loans to corporations.

Liabilities, the balances appearing on the top right-hand side of the balance sheet, represent obligations owed to outsiders. Accountants recognize liabilities when corporations receive something of value in exchange for a promise to pay money or provide goods or services.

Accountants value long-term financial obligations with predictable disbursements, such as bonds and lease contracts, as the sum of discounted future payments. As with assets, accountants classify liabilities in decreasing order of liquidity: Payables due within 30 days appear near the top while long-term bonds appear near the bottom.

Shareholders' equity, representing the difference between assets and liabilities, appears in U.S. balance sheets' lower right-hand corner and constitutes owners' residual claim on assets. An early classification issue was apportioning equity between investors' original capital contributions and retained earnings from subsequent operations. Firms generally could pay dividends only out of retained earnings.

Debt and shareholders' equity, collectively known as capital, make up a firm's long-term financing. Bondholders and stock investors trade divisible pieces of these balances in capital markets.

Railroads, heavy users of debt financing in the late 1800s, were the first American firms to issue balance sheets to absentee creditors. Balance sheets served as a tool to let bondholders evaluate stewardship and determine whether management stole or misused corporate assets.

Financial accounting's second major deliverable is the income statement. Revenue and expense accounts represent temporary extensions of the retained earnings section of shareholders' equity. Revenue shows increases and expenses show decreases in retained earnings within an accounting period.[6] Revenues arise from transactions that increase a company's assets. Expenses represent consumption of assets to bring in revenue. Any excess of revenues over expenses plus distributions to owners adds to retained earnings.

Just as historical cost represents the bedrock of asset valuation, matching is the foundation of the income statement. Instead of comparing inflows and outflows of cash, accountants use accruals to align efforts and accomplishments over an accounting period. Management estimates used to match revenues and expenses (e.g., provisions for bad debt, obsolete inventory, or future income taxes) convey information valuable to investors and creditors.

Perhaps the most important accounting decision a bookkeeper can make is determining whether resources consumed today will generate revenue in future accounting periods. If the answer is yes, then the charge should be *capitalized* and classified on the balance sheet as an asset. If not, then the balance should be *expensed*, flow through the income statement, and accumulate as a reduction in retained earnings. This issue will reappear in subsequent chapters.

The stylized income statement shown in Table 1.1 shows how revenues and expenses influence the retained earnings account in successive balance sheets. The excess of inflows over outflows provides a measure of income for one accounting period and attempts to identify the cash a firm can expect to realize from transactions reported in that period. No accounting theorist or practitioner has yet developed a widely accepted definition for *income* or *bottom line.*

With increasing stock ownership in the 1920s, the income statement displaced the balance sheet as the primary financial statement. Lenders want to know if they will get their money back. Balance sheets show potential collateral and existence of other claims. Shareholders care about a corporation's ability to pay future dividends through growth and improved margins. Whereas balance sheets supported creditor evaluation of management

Table 1.1   Income Statement Characterizes Changes
in Retained Earnings

Retained earnings, beginning of accounting period		$50,000
Sales revenue	$100,000	
Cost of goods sold	(60,000)	
Gross margin	40,000	
Selling and administrative expenses	(25,000)	
Pretax income	15,000	
Income taxes	(5,000)	
Income from continuing operations	**10,000**	
Nonrecurring income, net of taxes	2,000	
Net income	12,000	
Dividend declared to shareholders	(5,000)	
Increase in retained earnings	$7,000	7,000
Retained earnings, end of accounting period		$57,000

stewardship, income statements published by corporations in the early twentieth century allowed equity investors to value company shares.

Wall Street gravitated toward income from continuing operations, also frequently labeled with the non-GAAP term *operating income*—the $10,000 figure in Table 1.1—as the chief indicator of future earnings power and dividend capacity. Balance sheets came to be viewed as holding tanks of unallocated debits and credits yet to flow through future income statements. By the mid-twentieth century, U.S. corporate accounting's primary purpose was computation of earnings to facilitate stock valuation. Many investors multiplied current earnings by some valuation factor to arrive at an indicated share price. The relationship between accounting earnings and stock prices became the single most important association in U.S. security analysis.

During this time financial accounting began to serve a third purpose. In the most cited journal article in the history of finance, "Theory of the Firm," Michael Jensen and William Meckling showed that interests of employee-managers and outside investors could never be completely aligned. Even the most loyal employees' preferences differ from those of absentee investors. *Agency costs* represent investor losses sustained when employees act in unwanted ways.

Absentee ownership became synonymous with corporate America. Perhaps the first modern American corporation was the Boston Manufacturing Company, a textile firm organized in 1813. By 1830 ownership had spread from 11 to 76 shareholders. No shareholder controlled more than 8.5 percent of the company, and directors collectively held just 22 percent of the voting stock. No single owner could dictate company strategy. By 1930 the largest shareholder of AT&T, United States Steel, and the Pennsylvania Railroad each owned less than 1 percent of these firms' outstanding stock.[7]

Dispersed ownership means no individual shareholder can influence management actions, especially when management controls the proxy process for soliciting shareholder votes. Management abuses can easily arise from institutional separation of management from ownership: A notable example was RJR Nabisco's extravagant 1980s spending on a corporate aircraft fleet.

Investors and creditors fashioned contracts from financial accounting balances in attempts to align employee interests. Compensation schemes based on accounting results and bond covenants tied to earnings or debt levels were common examples. Regulators sometimes threatened intervention when reported capital levels dropped below agreed-upon solvency trigger points. Labor unions used reported earnings as a basis for contract negotiations. By the end of the twentieth century, reported earnings and debt levels became very significant issues to preparers of financial statements.

2

RAILROADS

President Andrew Jackson traveled and communicated no faster than Alexander the Great. Commerce's pace remained unchanged until the simultaneous nineteenth-century inventions of the locomotive and the telegraph. Railroad firms harnessed these technologies to create the first big, capital-intensive businesses. Such growth sparked the need for accounting's best-known dialect, financial accounting.

Someone seeking to travel from New York to San Francisco before the Civil War faced three awful choices. One could either travel cross-country by stagecoach, cross the disease-infested Panama isthmus, or make an excruciatingly long cruise around Cape Horn. Each took weeks and could cost thousands of dollars. Railroads cut the journey to one week and a hundred-dollar fare.

Historian Stephen Ambrose's *Nothing Like It in the World* recounts efforts of the Union Pacific and Central Pacific railroads to build the first transcontinental railroad in the 1860s. Smooth rails allowed trains to haul freight quickly at low marginal cost. The rub was the effort required to lay tracks with a grade of no more than 2 percent (106-foot rise per mile) and curvature of no more than 10 degrees (radius of 574 feet).[1]

Straight, level rails required ditches to be filled, passages cut, rivers bridged, and mountains tunneled. Each mile, using 2,250 ties and 9,000 spikes, crossed land often devoid of natural resources. Rail networks absorbed armies of surveyors, graders, and tracklayers. The Union Pacific supervised thousands of Civil War veterans using a paramilitary management model. Necessary labor, material, and transportation consumed unprecedented amounts of money.

Such sums brought trouble. Directors of the Union Pacific formed a separate company called Crédit Mobilier to oversee construction activity. Not dissimilar from an Enron special purpose entity, this enterprise was controlled by Union Pacific insiders so that transactions between the railroad and the construction firm could be orchestrated at artificial prices. Crédit Mobilier allowed directors to siphon money granted by the federal government. Financial scandal aside, the railway represented an engineering triumph.

By 1880 the U.S. railroad system had accumulated $4.6 billion of investment.[2] Expressed as a fraction of an estimated $11 billion nominal gross domestic product, railroad infrastructure had absorbed 40 percent of the American economy's annual output. In 2003 dollars, this would have been over $4 trillion, greater than the book value of the entire Fortune 500 at March 31, 2004.

No owner-manager could possibly front necessary balances. Railroads needed outside long-term financing. European investors stepped up, seeking a more stable political environment than available at home in the wake of the revolutions of 1848.[3] American railroads seemed to provide an attractive investment opportunity. By 1850 a few railroad securities traded on the NYSE; by 1869, the number had grown to 38.[4]

Railroads asked investment bankers to market bonds, preferred stock, and common stock to willing investors. Securities partition claims on corporate cash flows into divisible units that can be traded in secondary markets. Corporate capital structure, the combination of securities used to finance a business, establishes conditions and sequences for outsiders to receive cash distributions.

Bondholder claims precede those of preferred stockholders, and both precede those of common stockholders. Holders of common equity receive residual claims on corporate profits in exchange for voting rights to elect directors and approve changes to corporate charters. Corporate governance covers details of apportioning cash flows and voting rights among these claimants.

Nineteenth-century American industrial firms disclosed little to outsiders. Owner-managers saw little upside to sharing financial information, and they worried that disclosure could help competitors. In 1866 the Delaware, Lackawanna, and Western Rail Road Company treasurer replied to an NYSE information request by stating his managers make "no reports and publish no statements and have done nothing of the sort for the last five years." The New York Central and Hudson River Railroad did not issue an annual report to shareholders during the 1870s and 1880s.[5]

Railroads initially raised money without financial disclosure. Investors bought securities based on confidence in the investment banker. Bankers were supposed to undertake their own investigations before offering securities to the public. A prospectus describing the security could be as short as two pages.[6] An early specialty of JP Morgan bankers was marketing American railroad bonds to European investors.[7]

Distant investors sought additional information to assess

railroad performance. In the absence of accounting information, some investors looked at dividend payment rates. Cash can be a simple, visible, and credible indicator of operating health. However, dividends represent an imperfect signal because firms could dip into contributed capital when current earnings were insufficient to cover distributions.

Management duplicity could cause investors to confuse return of capital for return on capital. Concealment of losses represents the essence of accounting scandal. These actions caused investors to pay high stock prices for ventures that could not continue large dividend payments.[8] Early corporation laws developed to forbid dividend payments from contributed capital, requiring distributions to come from retained earnings.

Bondholders turned to credit reporting firms to assess railroads' ability and willingness to repay debt. In 1841 a New York dry goods merchant who had compiled customer records decided to sell this information to third parties. The organization became R. G. Dun and Company in 1859. Cincinnati's John Bradstreet formed a similar firm in 1849. In 1933 the two merged to become Dun & Bradstreet.[9]

Henry Poor became editor of the *American Railroad Journal* in 1849 and published systematic surveys of railroad assets, liabilities, and earnings. John Moody identified a market for credit information and initiated corporate bond ratings in 1909, rather late in the development of the railroad bond market. The Poor Company followed Moody's lead in 1916 and entered the bond rating business. The firm merged with Standard Statistics in 1941 to become Standard & Poor's.[10] Rating agencies rivaled investment banks as information sources.

Investors sought even more information to assess corporate performance. Enlightened managers simultaneously sought to reduce investor anxiety. Financial accounting emerged as a communications tool to meet both needs. Since nascent reporting practices could not provide all information investors sought, European investors favored lower-risk debt instead of equity securities.[11]

Outsiders discovered that railroads reported transactions in varied ways, confounding interfirm comparisons. Beginning in the 1880s some creditors hired British chartered accountants to come to the United States to audit management reports. Barrow, Wade, Guthrie & Company, the first English firm to establish a U.S. office, certified financial statements of the New York, Ontario, and Western Railway Company, the first American railroad to be audited.[12] In contrast to contemporary practice, early creditors paid auditors directly.

Two prominent auditors learned their trade as railroad bookkeepers. Charles Waldo Haskins (born 1852) worked as an accountant in the North River Construction Company, engaged to build the New York, West Shore, and Buffalo Railway. Upon completion, Haskins became the West Shore's general bookkeeper and disbursements auditor. Elijah Watt Sells (born 1858) worked for nearly 20 years in numerous railroads. The two met, worked for the federal government, and later established Haskins & Sells, the first major auditing firm founded by American accountants.

A Roman architect in the early Christian era opined that a wall's value should be determined after deducting one-eightieth for each year it had been standing.[13] However, not until the age of railroads did accountants formally consider depreciation. What distinguished railroads was the scope of fixed assets. Railroads employed more and longer-lived equipment than previous enterprises. Hauling freight brought wear and tear to locomotives, rail cars, and track. Equipment gradually lost productive capacity and needed to be replaced.

Depreciation, the consumption of long-term assets used in production, represents a financial reporting problem because it is never clear when the wear and tear takes place. Journalist Roger Lowenstein uses a newspaper delivery route example to illustrate this concept. To figure weekly earnings, the car's gasoline expenses should probably be deducted, but transmission repair costs should be spread over a longer horizon.[14]

How should management match revenues with expenses when a major resource consumed was ephemeral wear and tear on equipment? The railroad accounting convention had been to write off the original cost of an asset when it was removed from service instead of reporting gradual depreciation.

An example clarifies the idea. Suppose a railroad firm spent $50,000 in cash at the beginning of 1850 to buy a locomotive, used the equipment for five years, and then sold what was left of the machine for $10,000. To figure periodic income, the firm may use many defensible scenarios.

Table 2.1 presents four of many possibilities. The first assumes no provision for depreciation. The next three use various estimates for useful life and salvage value. Annual depreciation is simply the original cost, less anticipated salvage, divided by the number years in the engine's useful life.

Assume the locomotive generates $25,000 in revenue annually and incurs $10,000 in operating expenses. The loss on sale arises from subtracting the locomotive's book value ($50,000 purchase price less all accumulated depreciation charges incurred for the five years ending 1854) from the $10,000 sale proceeds. Table 2.2 incorporates these facts into the four scenarios.

Table 2.2 illustrates a critical lesson. Net income over a sufficiently long time period equals cash inflows minus cash outflows, other than transactions with owners.[15] Regardless of depreciation assumptions made, the locomotive generates $35,000 of income over its five-year life. With one notable exception discussed in the next chapter, accounting principles do not affect a corporation's

Table 2.1   Four of Many Possible Depreciation Scenarios

Scenario	Original Cost	Estimated Life	Estimated Salvage	Annual Depreciation
A	$50,000	N/A	N/A	None
B	50,000	10 years	$15,000	$3,500
C	50,000	8 years	10,000	5,000
D	50,000	6 years	5,000	7,500

Table 2.2   Equivalence of Depreciation Scenarios over Life of Asset

Scenario		1850	1851	1852	1853	1854	Cumulative
A	Revenue	$25,000	$25,000	$25,000	$25,000	$25,000	
	Expenses	(10,000)	(10,000)	(10,000)	(10,000)	(10,000)	
	Depreciation	–	–	–	–	–	
	Subtotal	15,000	15,000	15,000	15,000	15,000	
	Loss on sale	–	–	–	–	(40,000)	
	Income	$15,000	$15,000	$15,000	$15,000	($25,000)	$35,000
B	Revenue	$25,000	$25,000	$25,000	$25,000	$25,000	
	Expenses	(10,000)	(10,000)	(10,000)	(10,000)	(10,000)	
	Depreciation	(3,500)	(3,500)	(3,500)	(3,500)	(3,500)	
	Subtotal	11,500	11,500	11,500	11,500	11,500	
	Loss on sale	–	–	–	–	(22,500)	
	Income	$11,500	$11,500	$11,500	$11,500	($11,000)	$35,000
C	Revenue	$25,000	$25,000	$25,000	$25,000	$25,000	
	Expenses	(10,000)	(10,000)	(10,000)	(10,000)	(10,000)	
	Depreciation	(5,000)	(5,000)	(5,000)	(5,000)	(5,000)	
	Subtotal	10,000	10,000	10,000	10,000	10,000	
	Loss on sale	–	–	–	–	(15,000)	
	Income	$10,000	$10,000	$10,000	$10,000	($5,000)	$35,000
D	Revenue	$25,000	$25,000	$25,000	$25,000	$25,000	
	Expenses	(10,000)	(10,000)	(10,000)	(10,000)	(10,000)	
	Depreciation	(7,500)	(7,500)	(7,500)	(7,500)	(7,500)	
	Subtotal	7,500	7,500	7,500	7,500	7,500	
	Loss on sale	–	–	–	–	(2,500)	
	Income	$7,500	$7,500	$7,500	$7,500	$5,000	$35,000

19

cash flows. Depreciation merely reflects the arbitrary cost alloca-tions into accounting periods. Depreciation assumptions, and most other accounting disputes, matter little in the long-term course of business.

Few early statement preparers and users argued about depre-ciation. The concept was largely ignored until the 1909 corpo-rate income tax law permitted a deduction for depreciation charges in the calculation of taxable income. A 1916 Federal Trade Commission survey of 60,000 corporations showed that half did not include a clear provision for depreciation in finan-cial affairs.[16]

At the beginning of the twentieth century, some managers began to use depreciation to smooth reported earnings. A 1912 *Journal of Accountancy* editorial complained that depreciation had become a tool used by management to counter fluctuations in profits. Good years had been made to bear heavy charges. Bad years bore no provision or an inadequate one.[17]

By the late nineteenth century many farmers came to resent eco-nomic power held by railroads. Congress created the Interstate Commerce Commission (ICC) in 1887, the first federal regula-tory agency, to ensure shipping rates were published and fair. The ICC had little ability to accomplish its objectives until pas-sage of the 1906 Hepburn Act.

This Progressive legislation gave the ICC power to establish maximum shipping rates and required railroads to adopt uni-form accounting practices. Rules promulgated in 1907 by the ICC required railroads to charge the income statement with a provision for depreciation for certain classes of equipment, but lax enforcement continued up until 1943.[18]

Accounting rules resulting from the Hepburn Act were the first in U.S. history that could be enforced by federal law under penalty of fine or imprisonment for lack of compliance. Histori-ans found evidence that hostile rate regulation based on ac-counting measures of income created an incentive for managers to report lower earnings because income-based regulation penalizes better-performing firms.[19] Rules influenced management behavior when reporting results.

Other federal regulatory bodies such as the Federal Power Commission and the Federal Communications Commission subsequently emerged to set industry-specific accounting guidelines to promote interfirm financial comparisons and regulate prices.[20]

On March 12, 1903, United States Steel published consolidated financial statements as of December 31, 1902, together with Price Waterhouse & Company's assurance that they were *audited and found correct.*[21] Managing partner Arthur Lowes Dickinson insisted U.S. Steel present consolidated statements showing assets and liabilities of all subsidiary operations, instead of just the parent company's accounts.[22] The era of modern financial accounting had dawned.

3

TAXES

[T]here is nothing sinister in so arranging one's affairs as to keep taxes as low as possible.

—Learned Hand, *Commissioner v. Newman*,
159 F.2d 848 (1947)

Chapter 2 provided background for the development of financial accounting, a tool allowing outside creditors to monitor managers' use of corporate assets and enabling regulators to assess whether rates charged were fair. The messiness of depreciation foreshadowed more complex reporting problems like pensions and options. Not until tax law allowed a deduction for depreciation did railroads take this accrual seriously.

This chapter looks at government and corporate use of accounting to collect and monitor income taxes. Not surprisingly, public policy and business issues caused tax accounting to develop as a distinct dialect from financial accounting. The second part of the chapter discusses how practitioners struggled to reconcile the conflicting purposes of tax and financial accounting.

➤

Governments impose taxes to raise revenue, redistribute wealth, and encourage economic activity. Up until the end of the nineteenth century the U.S. government raised revenue from tariffs and excise taxes. State and local governments assessed property taxes. The 1862 Union government established the Bureau of Internal Revenue to assess personal and corporate income taxes to help finance the Civil War. The federal government allowed the measure to expire in 1872.

By the mid-1890s, corporations had replaced partnerships as the country's primary form of business association. Railroads' success created some extremely rich shareholders. An 1890 survey showed three of the four wealthiest families in the United States—the Vanderbilts, Goulds, and Stanfords—had roots in the railroad business.[1]

However, corporate efficiency depressed farmers' commodity prices and land values and prevented craftsmen from competing in scale-sensitive industries. Populist politicians acknowledged the disenfranchised and engendered anticorporate sentiment.

In 1893 the U.S. economy suffered another depression, and the federal government needed revenue to cover the tax shortfall. Higher tariffs would help domestic manufacturers but place a greater burden on the common man. A collection of Democrat and Populist legislators seized on a corporate income tax as a fair means of shifting the tax burden. The Revenue Act of 1894 provided for a flat 2 percent tax on corporate profits, defined as revenues (receipts, gains, and income) less operating expenses.

Three tenets of U.S. tax policy have been ability to pay, equality of sacrifice, and imposition of burdens commensurate with government benefits received.[2] Corporations had cash, had not paid taxes, and enjoyed protections offered by the federal government. If one considered a corporation a taxable entity, then the government could justifiably raise revenue through income taxation.

Chief Justice John Marshall, writing in the *Dartmouth* case, defined a corporation as a legal being. Where a partnership is a conduit to its owners, a corporation is an entity distinct from shareholders with its own records. Corporations, legislators reasoned, were fully capable of paying their own income taxes.

Figure 3.1 displays an image of Internal Revenue Form 366, describing revenues and expenses used to calculate corporate

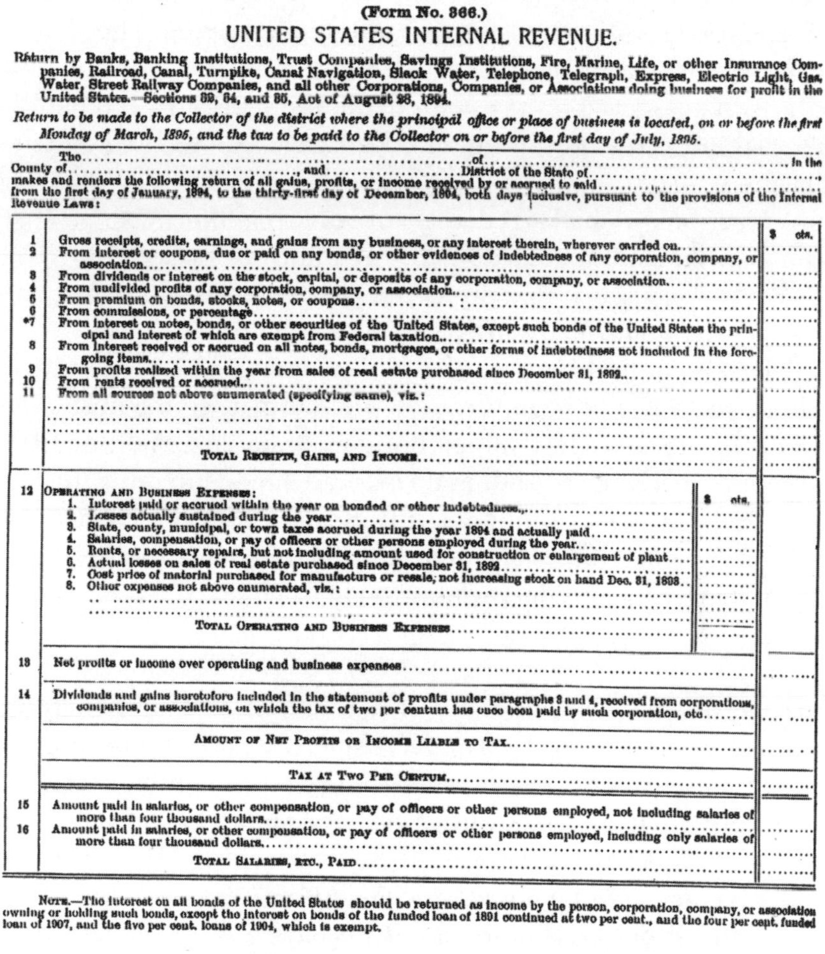

(Form No. 366.)

UNITED STATES INTERNAL REVENUE.

Return by Banks, Banking Institutions, Trust Companies, Savings Institutions, Fire, Marine, Life, or other Insurance Companies, Railroad, Canal, Turnpike, Canal Navigation, Slack Water, Telephone, Telegraph, Express, Electric Light, Gas, Water, Street Railway Companies, and all other Corporations, Companies, or Associations doing business for profit in the United States. Sections 33, 34, and 35, Act of August 28, 1894.

Return to be made to the Collector of the district where the principal office or place of business is located, on or before the first Monday of March, 1895, and the tax to be paid to the Collector on or before the first day of July, 1895.

The .... of .... in the County of ...., and .... District of the State of ...., makes and renders the following return of all gains, profits, or income received by or accrued to said .... from the first day of January, 1894, to the thirty-first day of December, 1894, both days inclusive, pursuant to the provisions of the Internal Revenue Laws:

		$ cts.
1	Gross receipts, credits, earnings, and gains from any business, or any interest therein, wherever carried on.	
2	From interest or coupons, due or paid on any bonds, or other evidences of indebtedness of any corporation, company, or association.	
3	From dividends or interest on the stock, capital, or deposits of any corporation, company, or association.	
4	From undivided profits of any corporation, company, or association.	
5	From premium on bonds, stocks, notes, or coupons.	
6	From commissions, or percentage.	
*7	From interest on notes, bonds, or other securities of the United States, except such bonds of the United States the principal and interest of which are exempt from Federal taxation.	
8	From interest received or accrued on all notes, bonds, mortgages, or other forms of indebtedness not included in the foregoing items.	
9	From profits realized within the year from sales of real estate purchased since December 31, 1892.	
10	From rents received or accrued.	
11	From all sources not above enumerated (specifying same), viz.:	
	TOTAL RECEIPTS, GAINS, AND INCOME.	
12	OPERATING AND BUSINESS EXPENSES: ($ cts.) 1. Interest paid or accrued within the year on bonded or other indebtedness. 2. Losses actually sustained during the year. 3. State, county, municipal, or town taxes accrued during the year 1894 and actually paid. 4. Salaries, compensation, or pay of officers or other persons employed during the year. 5. Rents, or necessary repairs, but not including amount used for construction or enlargement of plant. 6. Actual losses on sales of real estate purchased since December 31, 1892. 7. Cost price of material purchased for manufacture or resale, not increasing stock on hand Dec. 31, 1893. 8. Other expenses not above enumerated, viz.: TOTAL OPERATING AND BUSINESS EXPENSES.	
13	Net profits or income over operating and business expenses.	
14	Dividends and gains heretofore included in the statement of profits under paragraphs 3 and 4, received from corporations, companies, or associations, on which the tax of two per centum has once been paid by such corporation, etc.	
	AMOUNT OF NET PROFITS OR INCOME LIABLE TO TAX.	
	TAX AT TWO PER CENTUM.	
15	Amount paid in salaries, or other compensation, or pay of officers or other persons employed, not including salaries of more than four thousand dollars.	
16	Amount paid in salaries, or other compensation, or pay of officers or other persons employed, including only salaries of more than four thousand dollars.	
	TOTAL SALARIES, ETC., PAID.	

NOTE.—The interest on all bonds of the United States should be returned as income by the person, corporation, company, or association owning or holding such bonds, except the interest on bonds of the funded loan of 1891 continued at two per cent., and the four per cent. funded loan of 1907, and the five per cent. loans of 1904, which is exempt.

Figure 3.1 Internal Revenue Form 366

Source: Richard J. Joseph, *The Origins of the American Income Tax: The Revenue Act of 1894 and Its Aftermath* (Syracuse, NY: Syracuse University Press, 2004), p. 169.

taxable income under the 1894 Revenue Act. The first corporate income tax return was due Monday, March 4, 1895, and any tax payment owed was due Monday, July 1.

The return allowed a deduction for interest expense from debt financing but made no such provision for dividend payments to equity investors. This precedent would have profound implications for corporate financial management in the next century. Also of note is Line 14, which provided for a dividend deduction from intercorporate equity investments. The deduction was an early attempt to prevent taxing the same income more than once: the investee corporation presumably had already paid taxes on the income that gave rise to the dividend payment.

Antagonists challenged the corporate income tax. In 1895 the Supreme Court decided the income tax violated the U.S. Constitution's clause that direct federal taxation must be proportionate to population figures (Article 1, Section 9, Clause 4).

However, the 1894 Revenue Act resonated with certain legislators. In 1909 Taft administration legislators used the misnomer *excise tax* to resurrect a tax on corporate income. In 1913, Wyoming became the 36th and last state needed to ratify the Sixteenth Amendment to the Constitution. Congress then had the power to collect taxes on income without regard to apportionment or census considerations.

Where financial accounting's oral tradition had been handed down from master to apprentice, American tax accounting followed a highly scripted process. Tax laws originate in the House of Representatives, go to the Ways and Means Committee, and are then debated on the House floor. Surviving bills go to the Senate Finance Committee, which sends reports back to the Senate floor for debate and revision. Bills passed by the Senate go to a bicameral Conference Committee to iron out disagreement. Compromise bills return to the House and Senate for a vote. Surviving bills go to the president for a signature or veto. Legislators can override vetoes with two-thirds votes in each assembly.[3] The tax code changes every legislative session.

This exceedingly political process bred a maze of bright-line rules. The Internal Revenue Code documents the cumulative effects of these statutory revisions to U.S. tax law. In 1913 the Code had 14 pages;[4] by 2003 it had expanded to more than 10,000 and required Treasury regulations, judicial decisions, and bulletins to guide compliance. By one estimate, Treasury regulations alone add up to more than 80,000 pages.[5]

Financial accounting serves the needs of untold numbers of investors, creditors, and analysts. Federal income tax accounting serves just one user, the Internal Revenue Service (IRS). However, the IRS deals directly with more people than any other organization in the United States. It conducts financial transactions each year with virtually every adult and business while financing 95 percent of federal government activity.[6]

Another contrast with GAAP accounting is use of the U.S. court system to resolve tax disputes. Unhappy taxpayers may avail themselves to district courts or specialized U.S. Tax Courts. The appellate process can go all the way to the U.S. Supreme Court. Management, investors, and auditors have no such forum for resolving financial accounting disagreement.

Taxation makes the government an involuntary partner to a business enterprise. Taxes reduce a firm's value to shareholders. Management thus has a fiduciary obligation to shareholders to consider tax consequences of business decisions. An old saw describes tax management as pursuit of payments' three *Ls*: least, latest, and legal.

Financial accounting is about matching efforts and results. U.S. tax accounting turns on the realization principle: income should not be taxed until cash is available to pay liabilities. Tax authorities permit deferral of unrealized gains until cash is received to prevent involuntary asset liquidations or borrowings to pay taxes.[7] While there are some permanent differences between tax and GAAP income (e.g., municipal bonds' interest income and the dividends-received deduction mentioned earlier), the two accounting methods report comparable results over sufficiently long time periods.

In the interim, varied definitions of income gave rise to timing differences between GAAP and tax statements as of balance sheet dates. Financial accountants developed the concept of deferred tax assets and liabilities to reconcile four broad categories of timing differences. Table 3.1 shows how tax revenues can be recorded before or after GAAP recognizes revenue and how tax deductions can be taken before or after GAAP recognizes expenses.

To take one example, assume a magazine reader prepays a subscription. The publisher receives cash and incurs a nonmonetary liability to deliver magazines over the next 12 months. Since no service has been performed, the company does not yet recognize GAAP revenue. However, cash receipt triggers the obligation to pay income taxes immediately. By the end of the subscription year, income under tax and GAAP accounting evens out.

Transactions involving cash receipt before GAAP revenue recognition or expenses recognized before cash disbursement create deferred tax assets. These balances appear on the left-hand side of a balance sheet and can be considered nascent receivables from the U.S. government.

Transactions involving revenue recognized before cash re-

Table 3.1   Four Types of Timing Differences between GAAP and Tax Accounting

	Deferred Tax Assets	*Deferred Tax Liabilities*
Revenues	Cash received for magazine subscriptions before issues are published and distributed	Installment revenue recognized before cash is received from sale of equipment
Expenses	Expenses accrued for future warranty claims before cash is spent on repairs	Rent paid in advance of use of a building, leading to a tax deduction but not an expense
Income	Tax income > GAAP income	Tax income < GAAP income

ceipt or cash payment before use of goods and services give rise to deferred tax liabilities, a sum appearing on the balance sheet's right-hand side that can be considered a precursor for future tax payments to the IRS.

The complication is that firms often grow for extended periods. Accumulated deferred balances may increase indefinitely before realization of deferred assets or payment of deferred tax liabilities. Deferred tax balances defy simple classification.

Financial accountants have long argued how to recognize, value, and classify tax-related timing differences. In December 1944, the AICPA's Committee on Accounting Procedure (CAP) issued Bulletin 23, *Accounting for Income Taxes*. The Committee acknowledged differences between income calculated under financial accounting rules and under the Internal Revenue Code. It did not require use of deferred assets or liabilities. In fact, the Committee discouraged use of such accounting when differences would be expected to recur over comparatively long periods of time.

In December 1967, CAP's successor, the Accounting Principles Board (APB), issued Opinion 11, also titled *Accounting for Income Taxes*. The Board proclaimed matching to be the basic process of GAAP income determination. Calculation of income tax expense should include the tax effects of all revenue and expense transactions used to determine pretax financial accounting income.

Differences between income tax expenses on the GAAP income statements and tax payments currently due on the corporate tax returns should be posted to balance sheets and classified as either deferred charges or deferred credits. Nowhere in the Opinion did the Board define what these charges and credits represent. Accrual accounting had reached its high-water mark in the United States: the APB was more interested in matching revenues with expenses than in achieving clarity among balance sheet accounts.

Disenchantment with Opinion 11 caused the Financial Accounting Standards Board (FASB) to add income tax accounting to its agenda in 1982. Five years later the FASB issued Statement 96, once again titled *Accounting for Income Taxes.* Instead of trying to match revenues and expenses on the income statement, the Board said financial accounting's goal was to properly recognize income taxes payable or refundable on the balance sheet plus any deferred tax asset or liability as of the balance sheet date. Tax expense on the income statement was the plug required to equate any required balance sheet entries.

In contrast to Opinion 11, Statement 96 explicitly labeled deferred tax items as assets and liabilities. These balances represent sums that will eventually be recovered or paid. A notable difference between the two rules concerns accounting for tax loss carryforwards. If a firm reported a tax loss but was highly likely to report profits in future years, under Opinion 11 it could record an asset for the expected tax refund since the loss would be applied against income in future tax years. Statement 96's conservatism disallowed recognition of such an asset.

Unhappiness with Statement 96's complexity caused the FASB in February 1992 to issue Statement 109, titled (you guessed it) *Accounting for Income Taxes.* The Statement relaxed requirements for recognizing income tax assets and required a valuation allowance if it were more likely than not that some portion of the asset would not be realized. Some corporations used the newly created deferred tax asset valuation allowance as another tool to smooth reported earnings.

This sequence of events shows how a layperson could become frustrated with the financial accounting standards-setting process. Authorities issued four standards using the same title. In the case of recognizing a tax loss carryforward, Bulletin 24 instructed statement preparers to recognize a deferred tax asset if they wished, Opinion 11 said to do it if realization was certain beyond a reasonable doubt, Statement 96 said never to do it, and Statement 109 said always to do it.

Vacillation signaled lack of conviction of what financial accounting standards setters were trying to accomplish, an illustration of the point in Chapter 1 that there has been little consequence of reporting the same transaction in varied ways.

Tax accounting for inventory provided academics with a case study on the significance of financial accounting policies. On the world stage, U.S. financial accounting in the twentieth century had two distinct reporting principles: last-in, first-out (LIFO) inventory accounting, discussed here, and the pooling-of-interests method for business combinations discussed in Chapter 10.

There are many ways to match cost of inventory sold with sales revenue. A noteworthy comparison involves first-in, first-out (FIFO) and last-in, first-out (LIFO) cost flow assumptions. The FIFO method means that the oldest units placed in inventory are the first to be selected for sales or further processing. The LIFO method means the most recently added stocks are the first to be removed from inventory. An old accounting joke characterizes LIFO inventory as first in, still here.

Selection of LIFO versus FIFO did not depend on goods' physical flow through a production process. Rather, the choice turned on management's wishes for reporting taxable income. Consider the example shown in Table 3.2 of a coin dealer who purchases four identical gold coins in a period of rising gold prices. The dealer then sells one coin for $500. Under FIFO

Table 3.2 Under Inflation, LIFO Reduces Reported Earnings and Income Taxes

Coin #	Cost		FIFO	LIFO
1	$ 275*	Revenue	$500	$500
2	325	Cost of goods sold	(275)*	(400)**
3	350	Earnings before taxes	225	100
4	400**	Income taxes at 35%	(79)	(35)
	$1,350	Net income	$146	$ 65

cost flow, the dealer matches the sales price with the cost of the first unit purchased and, consequently, posts higher profits and larger valuation for the coins remaining in inventory. Under a LIFO flow assumption, the dealer matches revenue with the cost of the most recently purchased coin and reports lower profits, lower ending inventory valuation, and lower taxable income. Selection of LIFO over FIFO results in a tax deferral of $44 ($79 – $35).

No alchemy is at work here. All inventories available for sale must be allocated between the income statement and the balance sheet. Table 3.3 demonstrates how an increase in cost of goods sold recorded on the income statement must be offset by a decrease in ending inventory reported on the balance sheet.

In periods of rising prices, LIFO statements release more inventory dollars from the balance sheet to the income statement. Assuming inventory levels stay the same or grow, LIFO results in lower reported earnings, later tax payments, and closer matching of revenues with inventory replacement costs.

Unfortunately, LIFO use over prolonged periods of inflation causes less realistic valuation of inventory remaining on the balance sheet. Early LIFO adopters still have inventory valued at costs prevailing during World War II. Depletion of inventory at old costs, known as a LIFO layer liquidation, can cause spikes of artificially high earnings.

If management's goal is to report increasing earnings during periods of rising prices, then it should use FIFO. If management seeks to defer taxes and conserve cash, then it should use LIFO.

Table 3.3   Allocation of Cost of Goods Available
for Sale to Income Statement and Balance Sheet

| | Cost of Goods Available for Sale | | Income Statement | Balance Sheet |
	Beginning Inventory + Inventory Acquired	= Cost of Goods Sold	+ Ending Inventory
FIFO	$0	+ $1,350	= $275	+ $1,075
LIFO	$0	+ $1,350	= $400	+ $ 950

Ideally, management would prepare external financial reports under FIFO and tax returns under LIFO. The firm would show increasing earnings yet minimize taxes through matching of revenue with the most expensive inventory acquired. The real world is not so simple.

In the late 1800s some raw materials processors designated a *base stock* of inventory to be valued at a constant price. Additional inventory units acquired at recent prices were charged against revenue to mitigate paper profits and losses from fluctuating material costs. Base stock was the necessary, permanent level of inventory required to support expected levels of business volume. No profit or loss was recognized on base stock inventory until it was liquidated.[8]

Early federal income tax law required use of actual cost flows to calculate taxable income. The 1930 Supreme Court case *Lucas v. Kansas City Structural Steel Co.* (281 U.S. 264) upheld restrictions against the base stock method for calculating taxable income. Justice Louis Brandeis wrote that the federal income tax system requires gains or losses to be recognized in the year in which they are realized. He deemed the base stock's smoothing mechanism inconsistent with annual accounting flows required by Congress to calculate income taxes.

In 1938 Congress approved LIFO use for leather tanners and certain metals processors. Unlike the base stock method, LIFO defines inventory cost layers using both prices and quantities. That same year the Treasury Department's general counsel established a three-member committee to provide accounting advice for revisions to the tax code. One agenda item was whether to permit widespread LIFO adoption. Committee members were Haskins & Sells' Edward Kracke, Columbia University's Roy Kester, and SEC chief accountant Carman Blough.

Carman G. Blough, history's most credentialed accountant, emerged as a central figure of early U.S. accounting policy. Born in 1895, he lost his right arm in a railroad crossing accident, took up tennis, and made his college team. After earning CPA certification in Wisconsin, he worked in the state's Tax

Commission and Board of Public Affairs. He then taught accounting at two schools and joined the SEC in 1934 as a financial analyst.

The next year he became the Commission's first chief accountant. In 1938 he joined Arthur Andersen & Company and soon made partner. During World War II he resigned to work in the federal government's War Production Board. In 1944 he served as president of the American Accounting Association and became the AICPA's first full-time director of research, a position he held until 1961, which allowed him to support the AICPA's CAP and successor APB. He also served as an adjunct accounting professor at Columbia Business School.

While at the AICPA, he acted as the profession's Ann Landers, publishing a monthly column in the *Journal of Accountancy*, responding to members' questions about auditing and accounting concerns such as whether merchandise in transit should be included in inventory. Blough reappears in subsequent chapters.

Blough opposed LIFO because the cost flow assumption did not reflect actual inventory movement. Kracke favored acceptance and countered that since LIFO generally reduced reported profits, companies would be reluctant to adopt it for financial reporting purposes. Blough compromised and recommended that companies should be allowed to use LIFO if they used it for both tax and financial reporting.[9]

In the subsequent year Congress made LIFO available to all taxpayers and passed an act to consolidate and codify internal revenue laws. The Internal Revenue Code of 1939 summarized federal tax law in a (comparatively) orderly fashion. Subsequent regulations issued by the executive branch's Treasury Department and case law recorded by the judicial branch served to interpret Code provisions. Congress rewrote the Internal Revenue Code in 1954, introducing accelerated depreciation and creating sizable differences between GAAP and tax income, and again in 1986, when the Congress killed the investment tax credit.

Section 22(d)(2) of the 1939 Code captured Blough's compromise and allowed taxpayers to calculate taxable income using LIFO if the taxpayer has not used any other inventory valuation procedure "for credit purposes or for the purpose of reports to shareholders." In IRS vernacular, *credit purposes* meant financial reporting to bondholders and *reports to shareholders* meant financial reporting to equity investors.

The LIFO conformity rule represents a unique instance when the federal government coordinated policy for financial and tax accounting. The rule was carried forward as Section 472(c) of the rewritten 1954 and 1986 Internal Revenue Codes. No other country has had such a provision in its accounting rules or tax law.

A resulting problem was figuring out how to use LIFO in industries holding large numbers of diverse physical units. Ernst & Ernst partner Herb McAnly described a concept in a 1941 speech to Midwestern accountants where inventory layer increases or decreases could be measured in terms of total dollar value, not physical quantities of specific goods. Using the *dollar-value* LIFO technique a wholesaler or retailer with thousands of stock-keeping units could determine LIFO inventory valuation with just a handful of inventory pools. A 1947 Tax Court permitted widespread use of dollar-value LIFO.[10]

However, LIFO had a prominent critic. University of Michigan's William Paton charged in 1938 that LIFO represents a "device for equalizing earnings, to avoid showing in the periodic reports the severe fluctuations which are inherent in certain business fields. . . . Certainly, it is not good accounting to issue reports for a copper company, for example, that make it appear that the concern has the comparative stability of earning power of the American Telephone and Telegraph Co."[11] Earnings volatility would become the signature issue for the accounting scandals of 2002.

With a clear tax law and improved accounting techniques, profitable U.S. corporations facing price inflation could defer income tax payments if they were willing to report comparatively lower accounting earnings. What happened? Adoption of LIFO came slowly. Consistent with a fashion model's mantra that it's better to look good than feel good, corporations seemed reticent to sacrifice GAAP earnings numbers in order to save tax dollars.

In fact, some adopters encountering financial distress abandoned LIFO, presumably to boost reported earnings and avoid violating accounting-based debt covenants. In 1970 Chrysler switched back from LIFO to FIFO and recognized a $53 million favorable cumulative effect from the accounting change. Observers wondered whether stock investors saw through the accounting and understood that LIFO adopters are generally better off despite reporting lower earnings.

The first Arab oil embargo together with relaxation of 1971 wage and price controls sparked a dramatic acceleration in inflation in 1974. The economics favoring LIFO adoption became overwhelming, and a host of firms embraced the switch. Sun Oil and Texaco adopted LIFO, Kodak and DuPont expanded LIFO use, and General Electric chairman Reg Jones explained its significance in an address to New York security analysts.

In 1975 Shyam Sunder, a Carnegie-Mellon PhD who had joined the University of Chicago, published a study of stock price changes associated with firms that adopted LIFO during the period 1946 to 1966.[12] Using sophisticated statistical techniques, he found evidence of abnormal stock price increases during the 12-month period preceding LIFO adoption. An interpretation of these data is that investors rewarded firms expecting to pay lower taxes from anticipated conversion to LIFO.

Statistics show correlation but cannot prove causal relationships. Sunder's study was consistent with the argument that investors see through accounting convention when assessing a firm's cash-generating ability. The study suggested sensible managers concerned about their employer's stock price should forsake accounting earnings to boost cash flow through deferral of income tax payments. Subsequent studies provided supporting and confounding evidence of Sunder's conclusions: divining meaning from security price movements is a tricky business.

The second oil shock, in 1979, brought another inflation spike. More blue-chip firms such as American Hospital Supply, Eli Lilly, and Clorox adopted LIFO. One academic estimated in the early 1980s that continued FIFO use cost U.S. corporations additional income taxes equal to 1.5 percent of sales.[13]

The metal, petroleum, and motor vehicle industries accounted for the highest use of LIFO inventory valuation. The absence of general deflation since 1939 made LIFO adoption a rational strategy for most manufacturers and retailers. Manufacturers' failure to adopt LIFO puzzled researchers. One could argue FIFO users were more interested in reporting high earnings than conserving cash tax payments.

The 2004 edition of the AICPA's *Accounting Trends & Techniques* survey showed that out of a sample of 486 large, publicly traded firms that disclosed inventory accounting policy, just 251 (52 percent) used LIFO for some fraction of inventory accounting.[14]

To be fair, some firms had valid economic reasons for not adopting LIFO. Some non-LIFO firms could have an absence of taxable income. Inventory in some foreign subsidiaries could not be valued at LIFO. Electronics, communications, and technology industries experienced chronic price deflation, so LIFO adoption would have matched revenue with lower-cost inventory and accelerated tax payments. Cyclical businesses with wide inventory swings could occasionally dip into lower-cost LIFO layers and incur substantial, irregular tax liabilities. Companies with especially rapid inventory turnover or lean manufacturing techniques reap comparatively little benefit from LIFO adoption.

By the 1980s LIFO accounting lost significance as price inflation decelerated. Subsidiaries of Insilco (formerly the International Silver Company) used LIFO to prepare tax returns while the parent issued consolidated financial statements using FIFO flow assumptions. The IRS challenged Insilco and argued breach of the conformity rule. Both a 1979 tax court and a 1981 federal court held for Insilco's position. Beginning in 1981 the IRS allowed exceptions to the conformity rule.

Inventory valuation highlights another GAAP-tax accounting difference. After historical cost, financial accounting's most important precept for asset valuation is conservatism. In the presence of uncertainty, it is better to err on the side of reporting low asset values and income numbers. All accounting estimates are wrong. Overstatement of profits and asset values can give rise to actions resulting in bankruptcy. Understatement represents the lesser evil because subsequent adjustments merely provide a fortuitous valuation gain.[15]

In the context of inventory, conservatism emerged as the *lower of cost or market* rule. If management has evidence that inventory has sustained damage, obsolescence, or other impairment, then the inventory value under GAAP should be written down with the corresponding loss charged to the income statement.

In 1964, Thor Power Tool Company wrote down excess inventory to estimated net realizable value and continued to hold the goods available for sale. In conformance with GAAP, Thor charged the impairment against earnings. Thor then tried to carry the resulting tax loss back to offset 1963's taxable income. The IRS disallowed the deduction and argued that the impairment did not reflect Thor's 1964 income for tax purposes.

The dispute escalated to the U.S. Supreme Court. In *Thor Power Tool Co. v. Commissioner* (439 U.S. 522), the Court held in 1979 for the IRS. Justice Harry Blackmun, best known for writing the majority opinion for the landmark 1973 *Roe v. Wade* abortion rights case, had been a tax lawyer in Minneapolis. He opined that financial accounting's primary goal is to provide useful information to management, shareholders, creditors, and others properly interested in a firm's affairs. Tax accounting rules, by contrast, permit the IRS to collect revenue.

Blackmun reasoned that financial accounting should be conservative, with measurement error deliberately biased in the direction of understatement of income and assets. Tax accounting, in contrast, should protect the public treasury and improve the amount and timing of collections. The *contrariety* of tax and financial accounting objectives makes attempts to reconcile the two impossible.

4

COSTS

When you can measure what you are speaking about, and express it in numbers, you know something about it; but when you cannot measure it, when you cannot express it in numbers, your knowledge is of a meager and unsatisfactory kind.

—Lord Kelvin, *Popular Lectures and Addresses*, 1891–1894

Cost accounting, the third dialect, helps management ensure things are done in intended ways. Corporations prepare financial, tax, and regulatory accounting statements for external users. Cost accounting reports aid managers in decision making. In recent years the term *management accounting* has replaced the term *cost accounting*.

All successful organizations use numbers to manage performance. Congress's 1993 Government Performance and Results Act required federal agencies to establish objective, quantifiable performance measures.[1] Every baseball coach is numerate. The smallest nonprofit organization keeps track of cash receipts and service delivery.

Corporate managers use cost accounting information to value inventory (and thus calculate cost of goods sold), evaluate business unit performance, measure efficiency, and support ad hoc analyses such as determining whether to manufacture a new product. Outsiders seek uniform financial, tax, or regulatory information; internal managers embrace diverse ways of communicating cost information to control business activity.

In simplest terms, cost systems seek to detect or prevent problems. A fire alarm represents a metaphor for detection control. As shown in Table 4.1, two things can go wrong: the alarm can sound in the absence of smoke or fail to go off as fire envelops the building.

Every detection system, no matter how sophisticated, on occasion generates false alarms (which give rise to needless tampering) or fails to identify serious problems (while managers, in a figurative sense, continue to rearrange deck chairs on the *Titanic*). The North American Aerospace Defense Command, probably the most sophisticated monitoring system ever developed, has sustained both errors.

No control system can eliminate both shortcomings. If the objective is to reduce likelihood of unreported problems, then system modifications necessarily increase incidence of false alarms. Reduction of false alarms necessarily leads to increased likelihood of unreported problems.

Prevention controls attempt to mitigate problem emergence. The most basic is segregation of duties: decision-making and record-keeping responsibilities should rest with different people.

Table 4.1   Type 1 and Type 2 Errors
Plague All Detection Controls

	Alarm Sounds	*Alarm Does Not Sound*
Fire	Intended outcome	Type 2 error
No fire	Type 1 error	Intended outcome

Separation limits the likelihood of asset theft or reporting inaccurate results. A dispassionate accountant is more likely than a line manager to tell it like it is. However, collusive fraud can defeat any preventive control.

Management accountants have yet to rectify human nature. There is no absolute truth in financial reporting or tax compliance, and cost accounting leaves ample room for skepticism.

As documented in *Relevance Lost*, the most widely read history of the subject, cost accounting predated financial reporting in the United States. Textile manufacturers in the early 1800s used cost accounting to estimate labor and overhead costs of converting raw materials into finished yarn and fabric.[2] The Boston Manufacturing Company, cited earlier as the first modern U.S. corporation with decentralized ownership, began in 1817 to allocate indirect overhead costs to manufactured output. The next year the firm calculated cost of cloth by type.[3]

During the 1850s railroads pioneered modern management. Managers with little equity in their enterprises made operating decisions. Railroads were the first high-fixed-cost businesses. An estimated two-thirds of costs did not vary readily with traffic volume. Railroad executives such as Daniel McCallum and Albert Fink designed systems to control movement of trains and traffic to recover these costs.[4] Cost accounting tools gave rise to operating measures such as cost per ton-mile.

Nineteenth-century corporate giants focused on a single line of business, using scale and information to drive down manufacturing and distribution costs. Management accounting allowed executives to monitor performance of subordinate managers. Large retailers used accounting systems to compute product margins and stock turns. Steel companies used cost accounting to compare actual resource consumption with target values to identify unwelcome variances and improve efficiency.

Around 1900 a merger wave created large, complex organizations offering varied products. These firms integrated engineering, purchasing, manufacturing, and distribution activities. Without proper control systems, these corporations would have foundered in their complexity.

The DuPont Powder Company, formed in 1903, centralized manufacturing and distribution functions that had been performed by scores of specialized firms. DuPont combined margin and asset turnover figures to measure return on investment and thus business unit performance. DuPont management also created dedicated cost accounting reports for manufacturing, sales, and purchasing activities.

Planning and control information allowed the firm to grow in size and complexity. By 1920, DuPont had evolved into the first modern, decentralized, multidivisional corporation using earnings and investment figures to evaluate corporate investments. Its corporate staff replaced financial markets in making capital allocation decisions.

General Motors (GM), also created from a merger of smaller firms, did not have DuPont's administrative infrastructure. By 1920 GM faced myriad financial and operational problems. DuPont owned 23 percent of the car manufacturer and brought in Pierre DuPont and later Alfred P. Sloan to fix GM.

Within five years, GM had a sophisticated forecasting system to shield manufacturing from wide volume swings, flexible budgets to evaluate performance at varied levels of output, and an executive stock-based incentive plan based on divisional performance. Better controls permitted GM to increase annual inventory turns from 1.5 times in 1921 to 6.3 in 1925.[5] Faster turnover meant more efficient asset use to generate sales revenue.

Do cost accounting systems matter? A counterpoint to the GM case study was the experience of Ford Motor Company during this time. Henry Ford disdained accountants. GM flourished while Ford's market share slid from 60 percent at the end of World War I to under 20 percent 25 years later.[6] CEO Edsel Ford died unexpectedly in 1943 and father Henry was soon no longer capable of running the firm.

Twenty-eight-year-old Henry Ford II secured a release from

the Navy to run the family business in 1945. The company hadn't made money in decades. According to one story, things were so bad that the firm weighed unpaid invoices to estimate accounts payable. The private company retained Lybrand, Ross Bros. & Montgomery to prepare certified statements as of December 31, 1945. The auditors worked for a year and gave up.[7]

Young Henry realized he knew little of business administration and that the family firm was in shambles. Ten officers from the U.S. Army Air Force's Office of Statistical Control offered help and joined Ford in 1946. These men, in their twenties, came to be known as the Whiz Kids. The team created diagnostic measures to evaluate business unit performance and streamlined systems so new cars came to market faster. Ford Motor Company resumed making money and successfully went public in 1956.

Robert McNamara, best known of the group, had taught control at Harvard Business School for three years before the war. In 15 years at Ford he rose to serve briefly as president, before going on to be Defense Secretary under John F. Kennedy and Lyndon B. Johnson and then head of the World Bank. Arjay Miller also became a Ford president and then dean of Stanford Business School. J. Edward Lundy built Ford's finance function into one of the most respected in American business.

By 1925 management accounting development stalled. *Relevance Lost*'s authors concluded that at this point American industrial firms had developed virtually every management accounting procedure that would be known for the next 60 years.

Cost accounting was of tangential interest to the CPA community. Auditors need to know that inventory costs displayed on the balance sheet are proper in the aggregate. Any error distorts cost of goods sold and reported earnings. Generally accepted accounting principles (GAAP) merely require that inventory costs include direct materials and direct labor plus variable and fixed manufacturing overhead. By contrast, inventory costing in India and Chile includes just direct material and labor costs.[8]

During World War I the CPA trade magazine *Journal of Accountancy* did publish articles on Navy Yard cost accounting, construction records, cost determination for contract purposes, and so on.[9] Yet CPAs spent comparatively little effort refining cost accounting practices. Auditors wanted their clients to use simple, rational, and easily verifiable means to allocate indirect costs to inventory.

Refusal by CPAs to consider capitalization of imputed interest brought a dispute between auditors and cost accountants.[10] In 1919 the predecessor organization to the AICPA rejected a proposal to create a cost accounting section.[11] The schism resulted in formation of the National Association of Cost Accountants (NACA).

Led by Stuart McLeod, the NACA combined centralized control with decentralized chapter activities organized by city instead of state. McLeod established a competitive system among chapters where headquarters bestowed annual awards based on local achievements.[12] The NACA and its successor organizations the National Association of Accountants (NAA) and then the Institute of Management Accounting (IMA) served controllers, not auditors, and pursued education over lobbying.

In 1972 the NAA established its own credential, the certificate in management in accounting (CMA). Whereas the CPA exam focused on financial accounting, auditing, and business law, the CMA exam covered cost accounting, financial analysis, statistics, economics, banking, and other disciplines faced by controllers.

In 1981 the NAA introduced the first in a series of Statements on Management Accounting (SMAs), which were less prescriptive than financial accounting standards promulgated by the FASB. Classified under a five-part framework for management accounting, SMAs present IMA views on objectives, definitions, concepts, and management of cost accounting practices. SMAs cover recommended practices and techniques for issues such as implementing activity-based costing, control of fixed assets, and allocation of information systems costs.

➤

Cost accounting is the one dialect where practitioners listened to outside experts such as economists and engineers. The field's early intellectual home was the University of Chicago. John Maurice Clark taught an economics course on the nature of overhead costs and published course materials in a 1923 book.[13] The son of John Bates Clark, after whom the most prestigious American economics award is named, attained notoriety for development of the multiplier concept taught in introductory macroeconomics courses.

Clark studied the behavior of costs that could not be traced directly to products. In particular, railroads' so-called fixed costs and ability to add freight inexpensively piqued his interest. His economics training led him to attack cost accounting problems with marginal analysis, the differential cost incurred if a course of action is taken or rejected. Clark reached three important conclusions.

First, cost accounting differs from financial accounting. While the disciplines share some primary records, they serve distinct purposes. Financial accounting concerns itself with revenue and expense to calculate an absolute level of income available to pay dividends after an accounting period. Double-entry bookkeeping further serves as a modest control to protect assets. Cost accounting, Clark argued, furnishes management with information needed to establish efficiency standards and pricing policies.

Second, he emphasized that cost numbers are not absolute. For some decisions they matter a great deal, while in other situations the same costs may be irrelevant. Cost behavior also depends on time frame. Daily, weekly, seasonal, and annual horizons lead to different conclusions about resource consumption. Clark spent considerable effort reviewing railroad cost behavior. Using data filed with the Interstate Commerce Commission, he decomposed costs into fixed and variable components. He found that over sufficiently long horizons infrastructure investment represents a variable cost that grows just as fast as revenue.

Finally, Clark emphasized that managers need to think critically about capacity costs. Few services are used evenly over the course of a day, week, month, or year. It does not make sense to charge consumers the same price for electricity used during peak business as at night or for phone service during weekdays and weekends.

He asked who should pay for capacity costs when equipment stands ready to serve yet actual output may be next to nothing. Fire hydrants can represent a large part of a water company's investment yet use an insignificant share of output. Around this time GM developed standard costs estimated from forward-looking assumptions about capacity utilization to address this question.

In 1924 associate professor of accounting James O. McKinsey's *Managerial Accounting*, a compilation of course materials used over the previous five years at the University of Chicago was published. Whereas Clark gave an economic view of overhead costs and capacity management, McKinsey offered practical planning and budgeting tools to control business functions.

McKinsey agreed with Clark that cost and financial accounting represented distinct disciplines. In his preface, McKinsey conceded he made no attempt to distinguish accounting from statistical data. Much of the information used in controllership does not come from double-entry records.[14]

He argued that corporate structure involves delegation of executive duties. Control ensures assigned tasks are done in intended ways. The raw materials for this process are record-keeping standards established at the home office. McKinsey viewed accounting and statistical records as the guts of management. He gave examples of recommended reports to control corporate sales, purchasing, traffic, and manufacturing functions.

In 1926 McKinsey left the University of Chicago to found the consulting firm that bears his name. Each chapter of *Managerial Accounting* concluded with a case study where the student had to answer open-ended questions from limited information. Sixty years later, while an MBA student, I interviewed with McKinsey & Company and was posed comparable case studies.

Also during this time economists R. S. Edwards and Ronald Coase at the London School of Economics developed the concept of *opportunity cost* in business analysis.[15] Opportunity costs represent benefits forgone from failing to dedicate a scarce resource to its best use.

If a firm uses a valuable plot of owned land as a parking lot, the income statement would not show any rental cost. However, a good cost accountant would note that employee parking was not free. Allocating the land to parking could cause the company to forgo sale to a developer willing to pay top dollar. The difference between what the company earned letting employees park cars and what the company would have earned selling the parcel represents the land's opportunity cost.

Forward-looking analysis requires opportunity costs to be estimated and considered even though they fail to meet financial accounting's recognition criteria. A common use of opportunity cost is including a firm's cost of equity capital when evaluating investment decisions. Equity does not generate an accounting charge under GAAP, but this valuable resource has other possible uses.

Past, specialized investments that cannot be used for alternate purposes are considered *sunk costs*, where the opportunity cost is zero. Rent payments, depreciation, and other accounting charges associated with these specific assets should be included in financial statements. However, cost accountants properly exclude sunk costs from forward-looking analyses because no management action affects their value.

The same resource can represent either an opportunity cost or a sunk cost, depending on circumstances. An oft-cited example is determining the cost of meat in Wendy's chili. The fast-food chain grills patties in anticipation of hamburger orders. If orders do not materialize, the meat becomes too dry to serve in sandwiches.

With no alternate use, the beef can be crumbled and used to make chili. Overly cooked hamburger represents a sunk cost and adds little to the cost of preparing chili. However, if hamburger sales exceed expectations, then use of grilled beef in chili has an opportunity cost because the meat could have been used to make more hamburgers. Cost estimation does not have financial accounting's rigor.

In 1950, University of Chicago accounting professor William Vatter produced *Managerial Accounting,* another collection of lecture notes using the same title as had McKinsey.[16] Vatter focused on internal control, budgeting, product costing, and cost interpretation. The Inuit language apparently provides Eskimos with dozens of words for snow. Vatter showed how cost accountants use many descriptors for resource consumption. Costs can be fixed, variable, normalized, actual, imputed, sunk, direct, indirect, controllable, uncontrollable, and so on. Granularity brings precision.

In marked contrast to future Chicago professors, Vatter eschewed theory. He provided practical advice and illustrative case studies without textbook answers. He taught cost accounting students to use individual judgment when diving into details specific to an organization. Students should summarize measurable factors—to reduce subjectivity—before making decisions. For example, he felt it was crazy to set product prices from historical income statement aggregate costs.

Experts' next intellectual contribution to cost accounting was use of present value analysis. Investments involve time delays between outlays and returns. Actuarial literature had discussed the time value of money since the early 1800s, but it wasn't until the 1950s that engineering consultants applied this tool to compare certain cash disbursements with risky future receipts. The petroleum industry, with enormous exploration and production investments, was an early adopter of this tool.

A 1954 *Harvard Business Review* article discussed the need for a tool to evaluate capital expenditure proposals across varied sizes and horizons. The author surveyed methods used by 50 established companies and found a lack of defensible standards in American business. He pressed present value analysis as the measuring rod to compare, say, a $5,000 project earning $2,000 per year for three years with a $60,000 project offering $10,000 returns for 10 years.[17] Almost 50 years later, the Financial Accounting Standards Board issued Statement of Financial Accounting Concepts 7, *Using Cash Flow Information and Present Value in Accounting Measurements.*

In 1984 Harvard Business School published "Mayers Tap, Inc."[18] Using early software designed for personal computers, the case study allowed students to segregate a company's indirect costs into pools of the student's choosing and then experiment with various allocation methods. The exercise demonstrated how modest costing changes influence reported product profitability. Consider this simplified illustration shown in Figure 4.1 of a two-step allocation process.

The plant manufactures two products. Product 1 requires little setup, while product 2's tighter tolerances make it more difficult to meet customer specifications. The two product types consume equal quantities of machine time. Spreading indirect

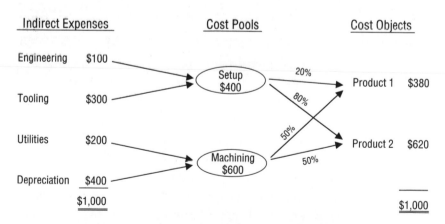

Figure 4.1   Stylized Activity-Based Costing Example

costs evenly to both products using customary allocation bases like machine hours or labor dollars could cause dysfunctional product costing.

Product 2's long setup time consumes more manufacturing resources. Failure to consider these costs could lead management to underprice the product, generate many orders, and forgo selling more of less costly product 1. A competitor with more accurate cost estimates would reduce its product 1 price and capture the industry's profits. Use of a proper two-step allocation system would have shown management a more realistic estimate of resources consumed to manufacture product 2.

Notice how a costing system merely adjusts allocation of known costs and does not affect quantities of resources consumed. In situations where organizations incur massive indirect expenses, allocation problems can easily lead to headline-making mistakes such as a hospital's $10 charge for an aspirin or a toolmaker's $5,000 invoice for a customized wrench.

Allocation principles really matter for large cost-plus contracts where the customer reimburses the contractor for resources consumed. The federal government has made extensive use of such contracts when purchasing complex military equipment from the defense industry. Contractors' inconsistent cost accounting practices foiled auditor efforts to evaluate allocations.

In 1968 Congress asked the Government Accounting Office to study the feasibility of establishing cost accounting standards to facilitate better negotiation and monitoring of defense procurement. Based on recommendations received, Congress formed the Cost Accounting Standards Board (CASB) two years later.

The CASB promulgated cost accounting standards as codified rules with the full force of law. These standards define cost terms rather than prescribe bright-line procedures for measurement and allocation. The CASB dissolved in 1980, but its standards continued to govern cost reporting for federal contracts.

Congress resurrected the CASB in 1988 as a function of the Office of Management and Budget. The CASB has five members who have exclusive authority to make or modify cost accounting

standards applied to sizable federal contracts. The 19 cost accounting standards in effect at the time of this writing cover topics such as allocation of home office and business unit expenses,
use of standard costs for direct materials and labor, depreciation,
and accounting for vacations and sick leave.

➤

Every control system brings unintended consequences. People
react to incentives in ways not contemplated by system designers.
One real-world disaster comes from the experience of Barbara
Toffler, a Harvard Business School professor who joined Arthur
Andersen's professional staff in the 1990s. She came to a firm using a product costing system designed to record revenues earned
and expenses incurred by nearly identical audit professionals
working out of various offices.

Andersen's convention was to credit all revenue to the office
doing the fieldwork. Should a partner in a different office sell
the business, that person was out of luck at year-end when performance evaluation and compensation decisions were made. As
Andersen grew and diversified, it did not adjust its costing system
to reflect the economics of more specialized consulting services.

A consequence was that rival partners fought over whose office's staffers did the work. Getting local hours billed became
more important than finding the best people to meet client
needs. The measurement system discouraged teamwork and rational business thought.[19] Perhaps the resulting pressure to bill
local staff time led to behaviors that sunk the firm in 2002.

Engineers use the term *suboptimization* to describe mindless
pursuit of one goal to the detriment of broader organizational
interests. An executive mandate to accelerate cycle time can lead
employees to sacrifice quality and cost control. Unhealthy focus
on a given goal can make an organization worse off.

In 1992, in a famous article, "The Balanced Scorecard," Harvard Business School professor Robert Kaplan and Massachusetts
consultant David Norton sought to address this problem. The authors likened a management information system to an airplane

cockpit's instrument cluster. Pilots need a holistic view of operating performance to keep the plane flying as intended. An especially well-defined control system reduces critical variables to a handful of measures that can be understood by all.

Balanced scorecards should consider customer perspectives (e.g., an airline's rates of on-time arrivals and lost baggage); internal processes (load factors achieved through better scheduling); innovation (ability to deploy new technology); as well as customary financial metrics (return on equity compared to its cost). The authors argued that traditional management accounting systems, sprung from finance functions to control behavior, fit the industrial age's engineering mentality, whereas balanced scorecards, giving primacy to strategy and vision, are suited to the kinds of organizations many companies are trying to become in the information age.[20]

5

DISCLOSURE

Publicity is justly commended as a remedy for social and industrial diseases. Sunlight is said to be the best of disinfectants; electric light the most efficient policeman. And publicity has already played an important part in the struggle against the Money Trust.

—Louis D. Brandeis, *Other People's Money*, 1914

F inancial accounting emerged as a tool that allowed distant creditors to monitor management stewardship of corporate assets. With the rise of equity ownership in the United States during the early twentieth century, investors began to use financial accounting for a second purpose, the valuation of shares. It's not clear that financial accounting was ever designed to aid investors in the forecasting of future earnings and cash flows. Nevertheless, financial accounting's ability to summarize myriad numbers into a handful of statistics proved alluring to stock investors. But when stock values crashed—and it became time to apportion blame—financial accounting received a comeuppance.

On October 28 and 29, 1929, the Dow Jones Industrial Average fell 23.1 percent. Investors lost billions. It wasn't until 1954,

25 years later, that the index returned to its 1929 peak. Recovery from the one-day October 19, 1987, 22.6 percent crash required two years. On September 17, 2001, following the 9/11 tragedy, the market lost 7.1 percent and recovered in four weeks.

The Great Depression's longevity spurred Congress to pass all sorts of legislation to prevent a recurrence. The resulting 1933 and 1934 Securities Acts forever changed U.S. corporate accounting.

In the first three decades of the twentieth century, improved financial reporting contributed to the public's increasing comfort with financial securities. The number of people investing in stocks increased from a half-million in 1900, out of a population of 76 million people, to 2 million in 1920, out of a population of 106 million.[1] Two researchers studying dividend income receipts on individual tax returns inferred that the number of stockholders in the late 1920s was perhaps 5.5 million out of a population of 120 million.[2]

Wider equity holdings brought ascendance of the income statement as the primary financial reporting tool. The income statement's emphasis on growth and profitability allowed better assessment of dividend prospects. Many publicly traded companies still chose not to publish income statements even though the New York Stock Exchange (NYSE) required quarterly statements from corporations listing after 1916.[3]

In the absence of income figures, investors turned to dividend payments as a crude signal of earning power. Unscrupulous managers could pay large early dividends out of contributed capital to give the impression of robust earnings. Nevertheless, declining dividend yields on common stock relative to cash yields on debt instruments provided evidence of increased investor confidence in common stocks.[4]

Critics spoke out in the 1920s against inadequate U.S. financial accounting. In 1927 William Z. Ripley, the Nathaniel Ropes Professor of Political Economy at Harvard, a chair later held by future Treasury Secretary and Harvard University president Lawrence Summers, wrote *Main Street and Wall Street*, the first corporate governance primer.

Ripley railed against inadequate disclosure—*publicity*, as it was then known. He argued that retail investors could not assess a company's earnings power without meaningful income statements. Firms did not disclose earnings or failed to do so on a timely basis. Before creation of the Securities and Exchange Commission (SEC), the NYSE was the de facto regulator of U.S. equity investing. Ripley made his point by summarizing data shown in Table 5.1 of firms' reporting intervals specified by listing agreements with the NYSE.[5]

He also criticized the absence of consistent financial accounting practices. Problems included use of depreciation reserves to smooth earnings, revaluing assets up from historical cost, inconsistent treatment of goodwill, and undisclosed debt. Lack of disclosure coupled with diverse accounting practices prevented Middle America from participating fairly in the stock market. Ripley believed the Federal Trade Commission (founded in 1914) should establish corporate financial accounting standards to level the playing field.

A second critic was NYSE staffer J. M. B. Hoxsey, best known for delivering a speech at the 1930 annual AICPA meeting in Colorado Springs.[6] Hoxsey argued that financial accounting's primary purpose had been to supply information to management

Table 5.1   Reporting Intervals of NYSE Company Listing Agreements, Circa 1926

Frequency	Firms	Distribution
Quarterly	242	25%
Semiannually	79	8
Annually	339	35
None specified	297	32
Total sample	957	100%

and creditors. Equity investors—his constituents—valued stocks on the basis of earnings, not assets. He criticized the conservative nature of creditor-based balance sheets.

Hoxsey implored auditors to influence their clients to report financial information fairly. Depreciation reported in an accounting period should be a function of infrastructure instead of current earnings. Engineers, not accountants, should dictate depreciation rates. Firms should issue consolidated statements showing liabilities and operating losses incurred by downstream subsidiaries.

Firms should also report sales revenue. Hoxsey acknowledged problems firms would encounter when such disclosure permitted customers to calculate margin figures. Disclosure might also bestow some advantage to competitors. However, no stock investor could possibly assess a firm's prospects without knowledge of current sales and profit figures. Hoxsey also criticized disclosures that failed to distinguish peripheral earnings from operating income, contributed capital from retained earnings, and cash dividends from stock dividends.

Adding to the chorus were Columbia law professor Adolf Berle and economics professor Gardiner Means, who criticized issuance of watered stock to favored investors. Most companies received cash in exchange for issuing shares. After 1912, some firms issued no-par common stock in exchange for dubious consideration.[7] The early meaning of par value was the amount of cash received. No-par stock could be issued for noncash consideration such as land, fixed assets, or worthless IOUs from subscribing investors. Watered stock diluted the interest of the old stockholders without providing the corporation meaningful new resources.

It is unlikely that financial accounting practices contributed to the Crash. John Kenneth Galbraith's famous study, written 25 years later, cited excessive speculation, margin loans, and market manipulation as causes of stock prices' extraordinary run-up in the late 1920s. He argued that the Crash represented bursting of a speculative bubble.[8]

In the 1970s, George Benston, a pioneer in the use of economics to study accounting, reviewed 1930s Congressional hearings and court decisions to evaluate securities fraud.[9] The transcripts revealed little reference to fraud or misrepresentation in connection with financial statements issued before the Crash. Legal cases showed few instances of fraud or gross negligence alleged against auditors.

He then reviewed stock returns of companies affected by a 1934 requirement to disclose sales data. Benston compared security returns for the one-third of firms that had not previously disclosed sales figures to the returns of firms that had. Benston reasoned that if required disclosure of sales data was meaningful to investors, then disclosure effects should be observable in stock prices after the rule became effective.

Statistical tests showed that the 1934 disclosure rule had no apparent value to investors. This finding does not mean investors didn't care about sales volume. Instead, investors probably had found surrogate measures to assess corporate growth. Later researchers found that security prices reflect economic changes well before publication of formal financial statements. Interestingly, though, NYSE stocks that issued higher-quality financial reports before the Crash subsequently experienced smaller price declines.[10]

Politicians sought legislation to eliminate speculative abuse. Price volatility affects investor confidence, business cycles, and tax collections. Well-functioning capital markets require the appearance of a level playing field. The two Securities Acts tried to solve these problems.

The 1933 Act became law on May 27 to "provide full and fair disclosure of the character of securities sold in interstate and foreign commerce and through the mails, and to prevent frauds in the sale thereof." On June 6 of the following year, the 1934 Act provided for regulation of securities trading in secondary markets and creation of the SEC.

Through the 1934 Act, Congress granted the SEC authority to prescribe financial accounting principles and specify the form and content of financial statements filed with the SEC. The House Energy and Commerce Committee has responsibility for federal securities law and SEC oversight. The House Subcommittee on Oversight and Investigation reviews the effectiveness and execution of these laws.

In one word, the SEC is about *disclosure.* The 1934 Act required public firms to issue periodic financial statements audited by independent accountants. Timely, accurate accounting disclosure was deemed a necessary condition for the proper functioning of capital markets.

The SEC also sought to narrow diversity of accounting practice. Its first substantive accounting move was publication of Accounting Series Release (ASR) 4 in April 1938. Any filed financial statements prepared in accordance with accounting principles for which there was no substantial authoritative support would be presumed by the SEC to be misleading regardless of the scope of supplemental disclosures.

In other words, the SEC gave itself the power to approve financial statements instead of just requiring their disclosure.[11] Two years later the SEC adopted Regulation S-X to codify instructions for the form and content of financial statements filed with the SEC.

Perhaps the best-known part of the 1934 Act was prohibiting company officers from buying or selling their employer's securities while in possession of material, nonpublic information. Executives did not have to disclose this information if they refrained from trading. If management sought to trade, then it had to disclose this information truthfully and broadly.

Disclosure matters because stock trading is a zero-sum game. Price movements create winners and losers. If a stock price shoots up, the most recent seller lost out on the appreciation. If a price tumbles, the most recent buyer gets stuck with the loss. Investors with an unfair edge could orchestrate substantial wealth transfer from the uninformed.

Wharton professor Craig MacKinlay offered the following illustration at a 2000 executive education seminar. Imagine you invested a dollar over the period January 1926 through June 2000 and could choose among three strategies: buy and hold government bonds, buy and hold a basket of stocks, or trade between the two asset classes monthly.

If you held bonds over this 75-year period, a $1 investment would have grown to $16 before taxes. Choosing the riskier basket of stocks would have resulted in a portfolio worth about $2,800. Albert Einstein marveled at the power of compound interest. Apparently he never heard of insider trading. With perfect information, monthly rebalancing would have grown the $1 investment at a 35 percent annual rate to $8.9 billion.[12]

Obviously no one has such information. However, a lucky few armed with better-than-average information could profit at the expense of less informed investors. Consider a stock[13] that does not pay dividends and had a $100 share price at the end of 1927. The stock price dropped to $50 over the next year from a bungled product launch and then rebounded to $100 at the end of the following year. Figure 5.1 shows that over this horizon the stock returned 0 percent.

Now contrast two investors who planned to invest $300 in the firm's stock. The first knew nothing about the launch and invested $200 immediately and the balance a year later. The second

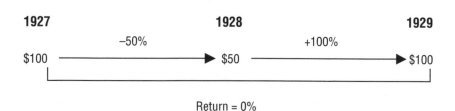

Return = 0%

**Figure 5.1   Return to Investor for a
Buy-and-Hold Strategy over Two Years**

heard rumblings about marketing turmoil and decided to begin with a more modest $100 initial investment. Even though the stock did not appreciate over the two-year horizon, Figure 5.2 shows how both investors trading within the shorter time frame made money.

Investor 2 modified investment timing on a piece of fuzzy information and earned enormous advantage over her uninformed colleague. A morsel of information may confer substantial benefit.

Congress promulgated the Securities Acts to raise investors' confidence in the fairness of U.S. financial markets. The SEC has subsequently sought to increase the volume and timeliness of accounting disclosure to further level the investing playing field. Interim financial reports provide investors with updated, condensed information to reduce the likelihood of insider trading over the course of a year.

The SEC did not require interim reporting until a 1945 program mandated disclosures about firms' transition to peacetime

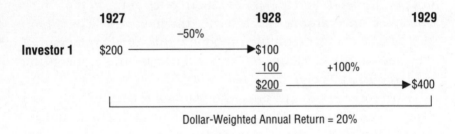

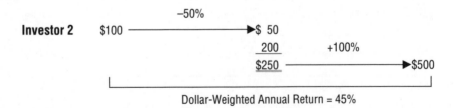

**Figure 5.2   Dollar-Weighted Returns of
Two Investors Trading over Two Years**

activities; it subsequently abandoned interim reporting requirements in 1952. Amendments to the 1934 Act passed in 1964 to regulate over-the-counter markets resurrected interim reporting. The SEC adopted the unaudited 10-Q quarterly reporting format in 1970. For the balance of the century, quarterly reporting was a North American custom.

There has been little study of the consequences of interim financial reporting. A theoretical model suggested more frequent reporting would improve the information content of securities prices, reduce volatility, and improve market liquidity. However, the model also suggested that increased reporting frequency creates more work for analysts.[14] Quarterly reporting became the central issue of financial accounting during the telecom bubble of the late 1990s.

Regulators did not consider quarterly disclosure to be sufficiently frequent. Private meetings between quarterly reporting dates could lead to the appearance of unfair access to information. To protect against selective disclosure to favored investors or analysts, the SEC promulgated Regulation FD in 2000. When a corporate insider discloses material, nonpublic information to people who may trade in the company's securities, then the company must promptly disclose the same information to all interested parties.

Industry associations sprouted in the nineteenth century to advance a profession's status and economic standing. Notable examples included the American Medical Association (formed in 1847), American Institute of Architects (1857), American Dental Association (1859), American Bankers Association (1875), and American Bar Association (1878). Trade groups enforced education requirements, professional certification, and a code of ethics. Many established lobbying offices in Washington.

The year 1931 saw creation of the Controllers Institute of America, formed to represent the interests of professionals who prepared financial statements. In addition to member education, the group embraced policy making and lobbying. The organization changed its name to the Financial Executives Institute in 1969 and then Financial Executives International (FEI) in 2000. Today the FEI is the leading trade group representing U.S. controllers, treasurers, and CFOs.

In 1937 a group of investors, including the legendary Benjamin Graham, formed the New York Society of Security Analysts to promote the intelligent use of financial statements to make investment decisions. The Society began publishing the *Analysts Journal*, later renamed *Financial Analysts Journal*, in 1945. Similar societies formed in other cities. Investors developed their own certification program, the Chartered Financial Analyst (CFA) credential, which required, among other things, a thorough understanding of financial accounting. Analyst societies and the administration of the CFA program came under auspices of the Association for Investment Management and Research in 1999.

In 1941 the Institute of Internal Auditors formed to advocate and promote the value internal auditors bring to their employers. Internal auditors are company employees who seek to verify the propriety of accounting balances prepared by colleagues and help senior management assess the adequacy of the company's control system. Under certain circumstances, internal auditors may assist CPAs in carrying out an independent audit.

Of all accountants (auditors, bookkeepers, controllers, industrial engineers, regulatory examiners, and tax managers), independent auditors worked hardest to promote their profession and secure public recognition. Public auditors in 1887 formed the American Association of Public Accountants, which ultimately became the AICPA.

CPAs lobbied for state certification (New York State, 1896; accepted countrywide in 1921); created a respected trade journal (*Journal of Accountancy*, 1905); required a college education (New York State, 1938); and established a uniform certification exam (1917, accepted countrywide 1952).[15] After the Crash, the Institute formed a committee and recommended to the NYSE five

standards associated with income determination and asset classification. No comparable trade group showed such initiative.

Effective April 1933 testimony of a Haskins & Sells partner
before the Senate Committee on Banking and Currency further
elevated CPA status. West Point alumnus Colonel Arthur H.
Carter, also president of the New York State Society of Certified
Public Accountants, gave the following testimony to skeptical
senators who believed government employees should audit corporate accounts.[16]

Senator Barkley:	Is there any relationship between your orga-nization with 2,000 members and the organi-zation of controllers, represented here yesterday with 2,000 members?
Mr. Carter:	None at all. We audit the controllers.
Senator Barkley:	You audit the controllers?
Mr. Carter:	Yes; the public accountant audits the con-troller's account.
Senator Barkley:	Who audits you?
Mr. Carter:	Our conscience.
Senator Barkley:	I am wondering whether after all a con-troller is not for all practical purposes the same as an auditor, and must he not know something about auditing?
Mr. Carter:	He is in the employ of the company. He is subject to the orders of his superiors.
Senator Barkley:	I understand. But he has got to know some-thing about auditing?
Mr. Carter:	Yes.
Senator Barkley:	He has got to know something about book-keeping?
Mr. Carter:	But he is not independent. . . .

Senator Reynolds:	Why should your members ask that they be permitted and empowered to check these accounts?
Mr. Carter:	Because it is generally regarded that an independent audit of any business is a good thing.
Senator Reynolds:	All right. Then, after it goes to the [Federal Trade] Commission, they have to check up to see who is right; they have to go through and audit again. There has to be a government audit, as suggested by Senator Barkley. Would it not be creating more difficulty and more expense and more time for the government if auditing organizations interest themselves in these various and sundry corporations? . . . Could they do it more economically than the government?
Mr. Carter:	I think so.
Senator Gore:	There would not be any doubt about that.
Senator Reynolds:	Why?
Mr. Carter:	We know the conditions of the accounts; we know the ramifications of the business; we know the pitfalls of the accounting structure that the company maintains.

In one stroke Colonel Carter accomplished two things: he kept the federal government out of corporate auditing and distinguished CPAs from controllers, academics, cost accountants, and internal auditors. In the federal government's mind, CPAs carried the profession's colors.

Further support for auditing was the 1938 McKesson & Robbins scandal, when a health care wholesaler created $19 million of fictitious receivables and inventory out of an $87 million balance sheet.[17] As an aside, 50 years later McKesson was involved in another accounting scandal that resulted in criminal convictions of several executives.

In hindsight, Price Waterhouse auditors failed to perform basic tests such as receivables confirmation and inventory inspection. However, public reaction to the 1938 scandal was that management could not be trusted to present accurate statements. Unaudited financials represented self-graded exams. Legislators and investors concluded that only attestation from independent accountants could validate management representations.

The American Accounting Association, National Association of Accountants, Controllers Institute, and Institute of Internal Auditors all failed to garner the respect earned by the AICPA. The investing public came to associate outside auditors with the accounting profession. Annually the master of ceremonies at the Academy Awards introduced the Price Waterhouse partner responsible for tabulating votes. The U.S. Postal Service issued a 1987 stamp to commemorate the Institute's centenary. No such recognition has been proposed for industrial engineers, tax preparers, or solvency examiners.

Auditor prominence created a double-edged sword. While CPAs established brand positioning as members of a learned profession, their promotion efforts inadvertently influenced public opinion. Investors came to believe that CPAs' primary obligation was to the investing public, not to the firm actually paying audit fees, and their purpose was to root out management fraud, not opine on whether balances were prepared in accordance with generally accepted accounting principles. This expectations gap would haunt the profession for the balance of the century.

Disgruntled investors who lost money came to believe they had a cause of action against outside auditors for monies lost. The reasoning was that the auditor had a duty to the investor, subsequent client financial problems not addressed by the auditor's report represented a breach of that duty, and loss on the investment constituted proximately caused damages. Since the issuing company often had no money, the investor's recourse was to turn to the successful CPA firm for restitution.

The concept of auditors' legal liability carried back to the English court system. British chartered accountants predated American CPAs. British auditors had a duty to perform work with the skill, care, and caution that a reasonably competent, careful, and cautious auditor would use. In the *Kingston Cotton Mill* case ([1896] 2 Ch. 279), an auditor took management's word instead of using physical inspection to verify inventory quantities and values. Because the client was a man of "high character and of unquestioned competence," an English court held the auditor had no duty to inspect inventory. An auditor was not bound to be a detective and approach his work with suspicion that something is wrong. He should be a watchdog, not a bloodhound.

American courts grappled with how to define the duty auditors owed to investors and creditors. On February 26, 1924, Touche, Niven & Company gave a clean audit opinion for the 1923 financial statements of rubber distributor Fred Stern & Company. Shoddy auditing prevented the CPA firm from discovering fictitious accounts receivable and inflated inventory values. In substance, the client was insolvent.

Stern then used the audited balance sheet to secure credit from Ultramares Corporation. Stern declared bankruptcy in January 1925, and the lender could not recover $165,000 in loans. Ultramares sued Touche to recover damages. One issue was whether the auditing firm owed a duty to a user of the auditor's report even though the user did not pay the CPA firm.

The New York Court of Appeals (*Ultramares Corporation v. Touche et al.*, 255 N.Y. 170) found that public accountants owe a duty to creditors and equity investors to provide audit certificates without fraud. However, liability does not arise from honest blunder. The case scared the public accounting profession because there is no bright line between simple error and reckless misstatement.

A second rude awakening was the Continental Vending case.

Lybrand, Ross Bros. & Montgomery signed off on client financial statements for the year ending September 30, 1962. The balance sheet included a large, questionable receivable from a related company. In substance, the CEO had borrowed company money to finance personal investments, something Adelphia's John Rigas would do 40 years later. The investments soured, and the executive could not repay the loan.

The 1934 Act made it a crime to cover up misleading financial statements. A jury convicted three auditors of signing off on Continental's financials when they knew the statements were misleading. That the accounts had been prepared in accordance with GAAP, where asset valuation requires judgment, did not constitute a sufficient defense. The appellate judge affirmed the decision after acknowledging the poignancy of convicting members of a respected profession who had led blameless lives. (*United States v. Simon*, 425 F.2d 796). In other words, you can comply with GAAP and still go to jail.

Threat of litigation against auditors escalated through the balance of the century. A prominent academic estimated that by 1993 legal costs for the largest public accounting firms amounted to between 10 percent and 15 percent of revenues.[18]

Public accountants coped with litigation risk by trying to reduce the scope of assurance given in an audit report. Since the 1934 Act, the CPAs' deliverable has changed from a *certificate* to a *report* to an *opinion*. This shift signifies a gradual attrition of responsibility for the veracity of financial statements.[19] Auditing firms also sought to avoid unlimited individual liability by adopting the limited liability partnership form.

Did all the legislation, regulations, and judicial decisions promulgated in the wake of the 1934 Act work? Historians and legal scholars have sufficient ammunition for unending debate. Former Comptroller General of the United States Charles A. Bowsher (schooled at accounting educations' twin pillars of the

Universities of Illinois and Chicago) commented that it wasn't until the 1970 Penn Central bankruptcy, 40 years after the Great Crash, that the United States sustained a major accounting failure.[20] The railroad had inflated earnings and paid high dividends to mask operating problems.[21] Four decades without a significant accounting scandal suggest Depression-era legislators did something right.

6

STANDARDS

*What has once been settled by a precedent will not be unsettled overnight,
for certainty and uniformity are gains not lightly to be sacrificed.*

—Benjamin N. Cardozo, *The Paradoxes
of Legal Science,* 1928

E quity investors grew disenchanted with diversity of practice within financial accounting. Accounting standards emerged to facilitate intercompany comparisons. In 2003 oil giants British Petroleum and ExxonMobil each reported $225 billion of revenue. One firm's revenue account included excise taxes to be handed over to tax authorities while the other excluded this pass-through item. Analyst adjustments prevented distortion in the prestigious annual *Fortune* sales ranking.[1] However, imagine problems assessing two start-ups' growth prospects if they report arcane pass-through balances differently. Discretion invites mischief.

Harvard Business School's Robert Anthony argued against a laissez-faire approach of allowing each corporation to set its own

71

accounting standards. Diversity of practice would result in much misunderstanding by the investing public. Without common ground rules and a general framework of accounting, financial statements issued by individual companies would not be comprehensible to many who used them.[2]

Regulators sided with Anthony. Resulting U.S. financial accounting standards described problems, discussed ways to solve them, and then prescribed solutions. Unfortunately, promulgated standards said little about how and why solutions were chosen. Comparable standards did not develop in other professions such as medicine, engineering, or architecture.[3] Even the American legal system rejected standards and used a combination of statutes, regulations, and case law to set boundaries for proper behavior. U.S. financial accounting standards promulgated since the Depression have satisfied few critics.

An early effort to forge uniform accounting practices came from the insurance industry. State insurance regulators created the National Association of Insurance Commissioners in 1871 to coordinate regulation of underwriters selling policies across state lines. The time lag between premium payment and receipt of claims settlements created a situation where regulation was deemed necessary to assure that customers' promised benefits would be paid.

The public policy concern was the winner's curse. Aggressive bidding by fire insurers would lead to insufficient collection of premium dollars to cover future claims costs. Local property insurers went bankrupt after significant fires in New York, Chicago, and Boston.[4] Uniform financial reporting could help state officials monitor insurance company solvency. Insurance regulatory accounting principles turned on liquidation accounting—how much could be realized to settle claims if all assets were quickly sold off—not on the GAAP concepts of indefinite life and going concern.

In 1916 the Federal Trade Commission chairman sent a letter to the AICPA to express dissatisfaction with the absence of uniform accounting practices and the apparent inadequacy of certain firms' depreciation charges. The government turned to auditors, not controllers, to effect change. Institute members contributed to a 14-page article published in the *Federal Reserve Bulletin* on April 1, 1917, five days before the United States declared war with Germany.

Federal Reserve involvement arose because member banks traded commercial paper issued by merchants and manufacturers. Buying banks relied on issuer balance sheets to assess credit risk. Reflecting the public accountants' bias, the article said little about accounting and focused on auditing techniques for verifying asset, liability, and equity balances.

In the early 1930s Price Waterhouse senior partner George O. May chaired a committee that worked with the NYSE to establish general principles for financial reporting. In 1934 the committee offered five guidelines for recognizing income and classifying assets.

The AICPA then formed the Committee on Accounting Procedure (CAP) in 1939 to issue Accounting Research Bulletins (ARBs). The initial committee had 18 representatives from public accounting firms, three academics (A. C. Littleton, William Paton, and Roy Kester), plus the SEC's Carman Blough. Notably absent was a controller from industry or a representative of the Bureau of Internal Revenue.

Just as World War II broke out in Europe, CAP issued its first substantive statement, Bulletin 2, *Unamortized Discount and Redemption Premium on Bonds Refunded.* The Committee was unable to select just one accounting treatment out of three proposed, a portent of things to come for the balance of the century. The very first U.S. attempt to reduce diversity of practice ratified the belief there was little consequence from reporting the same event in varied ways.

The Committee viewed its mission as narrowing accounting differences and inconsistencies. It never sought to push relentlessly for uniform practices, writing that while uniformity is a worthwhile goal, it should not be pursued to the exclusion of other traits sought in financial reporting. Diversity of practice was a necessary consequence of allowing new practices to be tried and adopted before precedents were discarded.[5]

The approach was shaped by May, Arthur Lowes Dickinson's protégé. Steeped in Price Waterhouse's British tradition of treating accounting as an extension of the law, May felt financial reporting should be governed by principles and professional judgment, not blind conformance with arbitrary rules.

A critic countered that CAP was in the business of putting out fires, not fire prevention.[6] Another charged that CAP never tried to define GAAP.[7] Bulletins were not based on formal research. Attempts to codify practice remained incomplete. Interestingly, just as CAP was formed, Congress and the Treasury Department managed to codify federal income tax accounting with issuance of the 1939 Internal Revenue Code.

From 1939 to 1959, CAP issued 51 Bulletins covering intangible assets, contingency reserves, income taxes, pension plans, and stock option compensation—hot topics that continue to this day. Unfortunately, no one was satisfied. The SEC was unhappy because of the continuing diversity of accounting standards. Academics were unhappy with Bulletins issued in the absence of a conceptual framework.

Among CPAs, Arthur Andersen & Co.'s Leonard Spacek emerged as CAP's most vocal critic. Andersen had earned fame as the auditor brought in to disentangle intercompany transactions of Samuel Insull's Chicago utility holding company empire. Andersen developed a substantial regulated utility practice and favored uniform accounting principles to facilitate comparisons for rate making.

Managing partner Spacek had gained notoriety as the only Andersen employee willing to stand up to founder Arthur E. Andersen. When challenged, Spacek showed his lack of fear by telling his boss he was from Iowa and could always return home to plow corn.[8] This moxie allowed Spacek to emerge as Mr. Andersen's successor and serve as the firm's leader from 1947 to

1970. The scrappy Midwesterner served as a foil to the genteel George May.

Spacek's experience with regulated utility accounting gave him strong conviction that fairness in financial accounting practices meant uniformity across firms. Using journalism as a metaphor, he commented that if someone read an article in one newspaper, the reader ought to be able to get somewhere near the same story from another newspaper.[9]

For the name Arthur Andersen & Co. to mean something, Spacek believed the firm must follow the same accounting principles in all client engagements. Accounting treatment should not depend on beliefs of the individual partner signing an opinion.[10] All auditors should reach the same conclusion given the same set of facts.[11]

Evidence that Spacek meant what he said was Andersen & Co.'s handling of the recently obtained DuPont audit. DuPont owned 23 percent of General Motors' stock and recognized income from GM's operations instead of waiting until GM declared dividends. While Spacek agreed with this treatment (eventually sanctioned by APB Opinion 18 in 1971 and later described as *look-through earnings* by Warren Buffett), the equity method was not part of GAAP at this time. At Spacek's urging, Arthur E. Andersen qualified the firm's opinion and promptly lost his prestigious audit client.[12] Comparable stubbornness caused the firm to lose railroad and savings and loan clients.[13]

Spacek had no love for New York colleagues running larger public accounting firms. He felt snubbed that his competitors considered Arthur Andersen & Co. a regional firm specializing in utility accounts. He also had little respect for the flexibility shown by the CAP. He once labeled CAP pronouncements as "generally accepted and antiquated accounting principles."[14]

In the 1950s, Spacek gave a series of inflammatory speeches criticizing his profession. It was unheard-of for a major figure to direct public criticism at both the auditing industry and the AICPA.[15] Spacek railed at CAP's closed-door proceedings and absence of documentation supporting Bulletins. He proposed creation of an accounting court to adjudicate disputes and document reasons supporting decisions.[16] Price Waterhouse and Haskins & Sells, serving commercial clients, emerged as leading defenders of flexibility.[17]

In October 1957, incoming AICPA president Alvin Jennings, managing partner of Lybrand, Ross Bros. & Montgomery, acknowledged problems with the state of financial reporting. He believed CAP had folded to industry pressure and failed to fashion proposals in the context of a framework. Jennings was concerned about the rival American Accounting Association's promulgation of theoretical accounting principles that were sometimes cited by the SEC's chief accountant as authoritative support.[18]

Jennings created a task force chaired by Weldon Powell, senior technical partner at Haskins & Sells. Joining Powell on the committee were Andrew Barr, SEC chief accountant, and Paul Grady, an executive partner at Price Waterhouse. All three men had been classmates at the University of Illinois and studied under Professor A. C. Littleton, an unrepentant defender of historical cost accounting and general principles induced from real-world examples. Powell was not swayed by the argument for uniformity at all cost: businesspeople should have the opportunity to experiment with different approaches to accounting problems.[19]

Committee work led to the launch of the Accounting Principles Board (APB) on September 1, 1959, to promulgate substantive rules based on accounting research. The APB would draw on resources of the newly created Accounting Research Division (ARD), designed to advance the science of accounting. These two organizations would collaborate to ensure that accounting standards were based on a rigorous foundation.

It didn't work. Both CAP and the APB were burdened with unworkably large boards of up to 21 part-time members who turned over annually. The SEC never endorsed the APB as the decision maker for U.S. accounting standards. The APB also drew criticism for private deliberation.

Most significantly, the APB ran into a buzz saw with issuance of its first significant Opinion. During the Kennedy administration, Congress passed the Revenue Act of 1962. A provision introduced the investment tax credit (ITC) to spur capital expenditures and economic growth. Firms buying qualifying property, plant, and equipment would receive an immediate tax credit based on the property's purchase price in the year of investment. Tax credits, dollar-for-dollar reductions in tax liabilities, represent more powerful incentives than simple deductions reducing taxable income.

The innovative ITC represented uncharted waters. Two rival accounting policies emerged, the deferral and flow-through methods. The deferral method viewed the ITC as a reduction in the cost of the asset and amortized the credit over the asset's useful life. The flow-through method considered the ITC a reduction in income tax expense in the year the investment was made and recognized the entire benefit in the year of property acquisition. Selection of accounting method does not affect cash flow. Profitable firms using the flow-through method simply report higher income in the year of purchase.

Table 6.1 serves as an illustration, where a firm buys $50,000 of qualifying equipment with a five-year useful life to earn a 7 percent credit.

Notice how choice of accounting method has no effect on cumulative net income, tax payments, or cash flows. Use of the flow-through method simply boosts reported net income in the year the firm acquired the qualifying property.

APB Opinion 2, issued in December 1962, required use of the deferral method and prohibited flow-through accounting. The APB reasoned that earnings arise from use of acquired assets instead of mere acquisition. Subsequent sale of qualifying assets would give rise to tax recapture, and realization depended on the business keeping assets in service. Therefore the deferral method better matched revenues and expenses.

Observers criticized the Financial Accounting Standards Board (FASB) for acting slowly and not pressing hard enough for uniform accounting principles. The APB passed these tests with flying colors. In terms of politics, the APB was tone-deaf.

Table 6.1 Accounting Treatment for ITC Affects Timing of Income Recognition, Not Cumulative Earnings

	1963	1964	1965	1966	1967	Cumulative
Deferral						
Earnings before taxes	$100,000	$100,000	$100,000	$100,000	$100,000	$500,000
Income taxes @ 35%	(35,000)	(35,000)	(35,000)	(35,000)	(35,000)	(175,000)
Subtotal	65,000	65,000	65,000	65,000	65,000	325,000
Amortized credit	700	700	700	700	700	3,500
Net income	$ 65,700	$ 65,700	$ 65,700	$ 65,700	$ 65,700	$328,500
Flow-Through						
Earnings before taxes	$100,000	$100,000	$100,000	$100,000	$100,000	$500,000
Income taxes @ 35%	(35,000)	(35,000)	(35,000)	(35,000)	(35,000)	(175,000)
Subtotal	65,000	65,000	65,000	65,000	65,000	325,000
Fully recognized credit	3,500	0	0	0	0	3,500
Net Income	$ 68,500	$ 65,000	$ 65,000	$ 65,000	$ 65,000	$328,500
Statutory tax liability	$(35,000)	$(35,000)	$(35,000)	$(35,000)	$(35,000)	$(175,000)
Credit on tax return	3,500	—	—	—	—	3,500
Tax payment to IRS	$(31,500)	$(35,000)	$(35,000)	$(35,000)	$(35,000)	$(171,500)

In 1973, just days after publication of the Trueblood Report on the objectives of financial statements (discussed shortly), Harvard Business School's David Hawkins argued in a speech that accounting principles should be consistent with national economic goals and government programs to achieve these goals.[20]

By denying business the immediate boost to reported income from the flow-through method, the APB appeared to blunt the ITC's effectiveness as a fiscal stimulus tool. The APB found itself at odds with national economic objectives because it did not recognize an obligation to help the federal government achieve fiscal goals.

In other words, Hawkins argued, accounting standards can never be neutral. Any standard influences behavior of statement preparers and users. If standards setters motivate behaviors at odds with government policy, the government has no choice but to take over the determination of these standards.

Reaction against APB Opinion 2 was immediate. Three of the Big Eight public accounting firms (Price Waterhouse & Co., Haskins & Sells, and Ernst & Ernst) told clients they would not enforce the standard.[21] In January 1963 the SEC issued Accounting Series Release 96 acknowledging diversity of opinion. The SEC said it would accept financial statements where the credit was accounted for using either method. This move clipped the nascent APB's wings and was unfair because the SEC had pushed for uniformity and then allowed diversity of practice on the first contested issue.

Outgunned, the APB issued Opinion 4 in March 1964, allowing firms to use either the deferral or the flow-through method. The APB in this Opinion conceded that its authority rested on general acceptability of published Opinions. Five of the APB's 20 members dissented with regard to the findings of Opinion 4.

Board member and SEC alumnus Carman Blough reiterated support for Opinion 2 and expressed doubt the APB could carry out its mission if it backed down when influential parties did not immediately accept an Opinion. Arthur Andersen's Spacek, another Board member, shared his belief that Opinion 4 illustrated

the accounting profession's complete failure to establish principles permitting statement users to make meaningful comparisons across industries and companies.

Tax accounting's political nature brings frequent change.
Congress suspended the ITC in 1966, restored it in 1967, abol-
ished it in 1969, and revived it in 1971. The APB tried again in
1971 to limit flow-through accounting in anticipation of the
ITC's return. A Senate committee noted in legislation leading to
the Revenue Act of 1971:

> The procedures employed in accounting for the investment credit
> in financial reports to shareholders, creditors, etc., can have a sig-
> nificant effect on reported net income and thus on economic re-
> covery. The committee, as was in the House, is concerned that the
> investment credit provided by the bill have as great a stimulative ef-
> fect of the economy as possible.[22]

Congress flexed its muscle and legislated "that no taxpayer
shall be required to use any particular method of accounting
for the credit for purposes of financial reports subject to the
jurisdiction of any federal agency or reports made to the federal agency."[23] Until the Tax Reform Act of 1986 eliminated
the ITC, a preponderance of firms qualifying for the ITC chose
the flow-through method in preparing financial accounting
statements.

The APB's companion Accounting Research Division (ARD)
experienced its own problems. It proposed a visionary accounting framework that challenged historical cost asset valuation and
matching of revenues with expenses on the income statement.
American business was not ready for the ARD's ideas on inflation
accounting, mark-to-market valuation, disclosure of holding
gains, and recognition of intangible assets. Statement preparers
and the APB ignored the ARD framework.

Despite these problems, one academic credits the APB with
two accomplishments. Opinions 3 and 19 led to widespread acceptance of a funds flow statement by public companies. Opin-

ions 9, 13, 28, and 30 clarified income statement classification so that financial statement users could distinguish results of operations from peripheral or transitory events.[24] These victories addressed classification, however, not the more difficult issues of recognition and valuation.

By 1970 the AICPA had lost confidence in the APB. The APB had failed to craft an accepted set of guiding principles, define terms such as *revenue* and *asset*, reduce diversity of accounting practices, or stand up to criticism from industry gadflies like Baruch College's Abraham Briloff, who argued that the absence of an accounting framework allowed financial statements to be incomprehensible to those who used them. Critics concluded that the APB lacked the mettle to create and enforce accounting uniformity.

In January 1971, the AICPA created two new task forces. Robert Trueblood, chairman of accounting firm Touche Ross, led a group to study the objectives of financial statements (Trueblood Committee). Trueblood had won the AICPA's 1941 Elijah Watt Sells Silver Medal for performance on the CPA exam. Former SEC commissioner Francis Wheat chaired a group designed to study the establishment of accounting principles (Wheat Committee).

The nine-member Trueblood Committee began work in October 1971 and did not issue its report until October 1973. The Committee conducted 50 interviews and held 35 meetings. When it issued its report, the Committee's sponsor was no longer responsible for accounting standards.[25]

The report concluded that financial statements provide useful information in decision making. Perhaps the most important information was that which helped investors and creditors predict the amount, timing, and certainty of a corporation's future cash flows. The report acknowledged that no one really knew how investors and creditors use accounting information to make these assessments.

The seven-member Wheat Committee wasted no time. The group formed in March 1971 and issued its report in March 1972. The Committee recommended moving standard setting from the AICPA to an independent organization. From this recommendation came the FASB, an independent organization comprised of seven paid, full-time employees, each working for a renewable five-year term. The SEC officially recognized the FASB through December 1973 issuance of Accounting Series Release 150. Neither CAP nor the APB received this seal of approval.

Board membership did not require CPA certification. The FASB also differed by following an exhaustive due diligence process based on the 1946 Federal Administrative Procedures Act, a procedural guide for federal agencies designed to solicit views of all interested parties.[26]

Once the FASB agrees to study an issue, it typically appoints a task force whose members have direct knowledge of the problem. The task force usually issues a Discussion Memorandum to define the problem and offer varied solutions. The FASB could then hold public hearings, solicit written comments, and release an Exposure Draft with a proposed accounting treatment. Interested parties submit written comments. If necessary the FASB could hold additional hearings.

The FASB could then issue a new Statement of Financial Accounting Standards to add to the body of GAAP or else table or terminate the project. It can take three years to complete this cycle. Some issues, like consolidation, have not been resolved since FASB inception. The good news is that the FASB process is deliberate and open.

Table 6.2 shows that standards setting bodies have learned from experience of predecessor organizations.

Academics and some practitioners had criticized the CAP and APB for promulgating standards without guiding principles. The absence of a theory can leave accounting rules up to politicians, where answers favor those in power. Many felt a strong theoretical base facilitates stable, consistent standards.

Immediately after its creation, the FASB embarked on a 20-

Table 6.2   Major U.S. Financial Accounting Standard Setting Bodies

	Committee on Accounting Procedure	Accounting Principles Board	Financial Accounting Standards Board
Time period	1939 to 1959	1959 to 1973	1973 to present
Number of standard setters	18 to 21	18 to 21	7, sometimes 6
CPA requirement	Yes	Yes	No
Paid, full-time job	No	No	Yes
Primary deliverable	51 Bulletins	31 Opinions	150+ Standards
Deliberation process	Modest	Significant	Exhaustive
Pronouncement	Suggestion	Recommendation	Rule

year, multimillion-dollar Conceptual Framework initiative to anchor U.S. financial accounting standards in defensible principles. Yet the FASB learned early on that it serves at the pleasure of the SEC, a federal administrative agency created by Congress. Politicians serve constituents, not theories.

One lesson concerned troubled debt restructuring. Economic weakness following the 1973 Arab oil embargo caused many loans to sour. Major borrowers included New York City, whose deputy mayor for finance, Sandy Burton, was a former SEC chief accountant. Lending banks often granted concessions to troubled borrowers to increase likelihood of loan recovery. Debt restructuring made the short list of FASB projects by the mid-1970s.

Suppose a bank loans $1,000 with 10 percent interest due annually and principal repayment in five years' time. Soon after receiving the money, the borrower experiences financial difficulties and asks for lenient repayment terms. As presented in Table 6.3, the bank, seeking to protect its investment, agrees to waive one annual interest payment and give the borrower a one-year grace period for remaining payments.

Term modifications shaved $174 ($1,000 – $826) from the loan value, assuming a constant 10 percent discount rate. Recognizing

Table 6.3   Debt Restructuring Reduces a Loan's Value and Effective Interest Rate

	Original Loan Terms			Restructured Loan Terms		
Year	Scheduled Receipt	Discount Factor	Present Value	Scheduled Receipt	Discount Factor	Present Value
1	$ 100	0.9091	$ 91	$ —	0.9091	$ —
2	100	0.8264	83	—	0.8264	—
3	100	0.7513	75	100	0.7513	75
4	100	0.6830	68	100	0.6830	68
5	1,100	0.6209	683	100	0.6209	62
6				1,100	0.5645	621
			$1,000	$1,400		$826

Loan's internal rate of return (IRR) 10.0%   Restructured loan's IRR 6.3%

84

the loss would reduce the bank's shareholders' equity. Regulated banks must satisfy capital adequacy requirements to stay in business. Taking too many charges could impair a bank's ability to continue making loans.

In July 1976, as part of its deliberation process, the FASB heard testimony from leading bankers in New York City. Citibank's Walter Wriston served as leadoff hitter, arguing forcefully that a tough accounting standard would force lenders to take substantial hits to their income statements when they restructured troubled loans. These banks would then become more conservative with loans to nonprime borrowers. Financially burdened cities, real estate developers, and minority businesses would subsequently have less access to credit.[27]

The FASB listened and issued Statement 15, *Accounting by Debtors and Creditors for Troubled Debt Restructurings*. Seeking to show that the economics of the deal changed but reluctant to force lenders to take a charge to earnings, the FASB concluded that changing loan terms did not represent a new transaction.

So long as the undiscounted interest and principal payments added up to at least the carrying amount of the loan (the $1,400 in rescheduled payments exceeded the $1,000 loan book value), the lender would simply recognize lower interest income (6.3 percent effective rate vs. 10 percent before the restructuring) and avoid posting a loss to the income statement.

Writing with hindsight in 2001, authors of a leading accounting textbook believed promulgation of this convoluted standard, which deferred recognition of losses and allowed thrifts to hide bad loans, facilitated an even larger 1980s savings and loan crisis that cost taxpayers billions of dollars.[28] Seemingly innocent accounting decisions can have large, unintended consequences.

A second triumph of politics came with accounting for oil and gas exploration. The 1973 oil embargo tripled prices and made domestic exploration more cost-effective. Large, diversified oil companies used *successful efforts* accounting and charged dry holes' exploration costs to the income statement.

Smaller exploration firms used *full cost* accounting and capitalized costs of both successful and unsuccessful well exploration. About 1 in 30 new fields in the continental United States at the time became commercially viable.[29] Wildcatters argued that dry holes are a necessary cost of discovering productive wells. Capitalizing and gradually expensing exploration charges provides a smoother earnings trajectory.

Once again, selection of accounting method had no effect on a company's cash flows. Over time the two procedures would show the same cumulative earnings. Simply drilling more wells in an accounting period reduces earnings volatility, much like adding stocks reduces variance of a portfolio's returns.[30] Smaller firms simply could not afford to drill as many holes as larger competitors.

The SEC had charged the FASB with reducing diversity in accounting practices. Issuance of Statement 19, *Financial Accounting and Reporting by Oil and Gas Producing Companies*, in December 1977 was consistent with this mandate. The FASB required oil and gas companies to use successful efforts accounting.

Small companies protested, threatened to reduce exploration to avoid earnings volatility, and lobbied Congress and other federal agencies for help. A Department of Energy official believed that smaller companies would reduce oil and gas exploration for fear of reporting unfavorable earnings trends, and the Justice Department asked the SEC to postpone adoption for fear of reduced industry competition.[31] Under pressure, the SEC issued ASR 253 in August 1978 and permitted registrants to use full cost accounting.

Just as the APB had to reverse its position on accounting for the investment tax credit, the FASB had no choice but to issue Statement 25, *Suspension of Certain Accounting Requirements for Oil and Gas Producing Companies*, in February 1979 and allow both methods. The SEC even took a crack at forming its own accounting method, reserve recognition accounting, but abandoned the effort due to implementation complexity.

The APB and FASB received the same message from the

federal government: reduce diversity of practice without alienating constituents. The fact that selection of most accounting principles makes no difference over the long run held no sway in politics.

Despite early triumphs of politics over reason, the FASB has proved more durable than the CAP (20-year life) and APB (14 years) combined. The FASB serves at the pleasure of the SEC and has been adept at consulting with this administrative agency as part of its due process. In contrast, the APB had brusquely rejected flow-through accounting despite SEC overtures to consider the flow-through method. One observer attributes FASB success to its willingness to act as a heat shield for the SEC, entering controversial debates and absorbing resulting criticism.[32]

The volume of accounting rules continues to rise with little sign of abatement. A pernicious consequence has been the changing nature of accounting education. A review of any intermediate financial accounting textbook published since 1980 shows the weight attached to teaching specific rules instead of general principles.

One professor bemoaned that accounting students learn procedures instead of how to think about issues. Formal standards, he argued, are a godsend to feeble teachers who find it easier to recite a creed than analyze facts and engage in argument.[33] Law students, by contrast, learn to challenge precedent and save memorization for the bar exam.

Perhaps a cause of all these rules was an attempt by auditors to get the opportunity to say "our hands are tied" in the face of management challenge to a recommended accounting treatment. Strict standards could mitigate opinion shopping from rival auditing firms.[34] Compliance with bright-line rules could also limit expansion of auditor professional liability.

Even with identical financial accounting standards, public companies must use firm-specific estimates to account for depreciation, pension and retirement obligations, deferred taxes, warranty expenses, and bad debt. Judgment can never be removed from bookkeeping.

As long as corporations use well-established principles, the specifics may not matter. A researcher compared bid-ask spreads (a measure of undesirable information asymmetry among buyers and sellers) and turnover statistics (a measure of desirable share liquidity) for stocks listed on the Frankfurt Stock Exchange's New Market in 1999. Listing firms could prepare financial statements in accordance with International Accounting Standards (IAS) or U.S. GAAP. Better disclosure should bring tighter spreads and higher liquidity.

There was little evidence U.S. GAAP provided superior disclosure to IAS. However, both accounting frameworks appeared superior to German principles: New Market firms using GAAP or IAS had stocks exhibiting 24 percent lower spreads and 30 percent higher turnover than shares for comparable firms reporting under German rules.[35] A well-established accounting system such as GAAP or IAS should do just fine meeting outsiders' needs. As discussed in subsequent chapters, the problem has not been with the rules but rather with the behavior of statement preparers.

7

SCIENCE

All models are wrong. Some are useful.

—University of Wisconsin
Professor George E. P. Box

As discussion over financial accounting standards developed, academics struggled for voice. Industry critic Professor Abraham Briloff lamented that the debate over public versus private sector standards setting did not involve the excluded middle of academia.[1] Over time, academics developed tools to help practitioners frame financial accounting debate.

Until the twentieth century, accounting education fell into the realm of commercial arithmetic, penmanship, and business letter writing.[2] In 1881 a Philadelphia entrepreneur gave money to found the Wharton School at the University of Pennsylvania, the world's first collegiate school of business, when there was no such thing as a business textbook or case study.

In 1883 Wharton offered the first college accounting course, which included a lecture series on "The Theory and Practice of Accounting."[3] Dartmouth created the Amos Tuck School of Administration and Finance in 1900, the first graduate school of management. Accounting was not part of its original curriculum.

In 1900 William Morse Cole offered an accounting course in the Harvard College economics department as a vocational aid for liberal arts students expecting to enter business upon graduation. The next year a half-credit was granted; in 1905, a full credit. When the Harvard Graduate School of Business Administration opened in 1908, the course became one of three required classes, together with contracts and marketing.[4]

Also in 1900 Charles Waldo Haskins co-founded, with Elijah Watt Sells, New York University's School of Commerce, Accounts, and Finance. The AICPA supported this effort and provided an early scholarship fund. Haskins served as its first dean and established the first professorships in accounting.

Early twentieth-century texts added intellectual rigor: Robert Montgomery's U.S. edition of Dicksee's *Auditing* (1905), Charles Ezra Sprague's *The Philosophy of Accounts* (1908), William Morse Cole's *Accounts—Their Construction and Interpretation* (1908), and Henry Rand Hatfield's *Modern Accounting* (1909).[5]

In 1908 Northwestern University opened a School of Commerce as an evening program in downtown Chicago. The next year a young CPA named Arthur E. Andersen joined as a lecturer. Andersen became Northwestern's first tenured accounting professor and formed an auditing firm bearing his name. Nearly 40 other universities opened commerce or business schools by 1915.[6] The University of Illinois granted the first PhD in accounting in 1939.

The first prominent accounting teachers, Ananias Charles (A. C.) Littleton and William Paton, put a Midwestern stamp on accounting education. At this time educating investment bankers was the preserve of the Ivy League, while accounting education was largely a Big Ten production.

Littleton, born 1886, graduated from Bloomington High School in downstate Illinois and worked for two years at the

Chicago & Alton Railroad. He then earned three degrees from the University of Illinois, joined the faculty, and founded the University's graduate accounting program. By 1952, when he retired, the University had granted 225 master's degrees and 26 PhD's in accounting. Littleton had supervised one-third of the University's master's theses and 90 percent of PhD dissertations.

William Paton, born in 1889, grew up in rural Michigan, attended the University of Michigan, and began a teaching career that spanned the period from 1914 to 1958. In 1915 a group of accounting teachers attending the American Economic Association's annual conference met privately to coordinate development of accounting curricula.

The next year Paton helped found the American Association of University Instructors in Accounting, which changed its name in 1935 to the American Accounting Association (AAA). Paton served as the Association's first journal editor. He wrote scores of books, monographs, and articles. To commemorate the AICPA's 1987 centennial, he was designated the Outstanding Educator of the Century.

In 1923 the University of Chicago's James O. McKinsey recommended that the AAA formally break ranks with the American Economic Association and hold its annual conference independently. The AAA spoke out against the 1920s corporate practice of writing up property values above cost.

In 1936, soon after formation of the SEC, the AAA published *A Tentative Statement of Accounting Principles.* Notable precepts were that transactions should be recorded at *cost* rather than *value* and balance sheets should distinguish paid-in capital from retained earnings.[7] This treatise represented the first effort by a U.S. accounting organization to document a coordinated set of accounting principles.

The rival AICPA did not respond to the *Tentative Statement.* The auditors' periodical, the *Journal of Accountancy,* did not even mention the document. The AAA revised its treatise in 1941, 1948, 1957, and 1966. Neither practicing accountants nor SEC staff members seemed to care. Members of the AAA also published theoretical monographs on topics such as inflation accounting and the philosophy of auditing. Berkeley's Maurice Moonitz, writing in 1974, conceded that all of the AAA's writing had little direct influence on the practicing arm of accounting.[8]

The AICPA formed its Committee on Accounting Procedure in 1939, sponsored by Price Waterhouse's George O. May. May rejected the AAA's approach of solving accounting problems from guiding principles; instead, he chose to take a common-law approach of publishing Bulletins based on specific issues.[9]

In January 1940, Paton and Littleton's *An Introduction to Corporate Accounting Standards* was published. The monograph advocated fundamental ideas rather than specific standards. The authors believed financial statements' purpose was to provide dependable information about a corporation's earnings power through proper matching of efforts and accomplishments. Responsibility for fairness fell on the shoulders of the independent auditor. The monograph was the only AAA publication ever to be read widely by practitioners.[10]

After World War II, Harvard Business School (HBS) combined its first-year accounting and statistics classes to create a required first-year course called Control. The syllabus emphasized use of figures and accounts for governing purposes and securing an understanding of their limitations as data supporting administrative decisions.[11] Where most schools embraced an external, financial accounting perspective, HBS chose to emphasize an internal, cost accounting approach.

In 1959 the Carnegie Foundation published *The Education of American Businessmen* and the Ford Foundation published *Higher Education for Business*. Each study criticized business education as too technical and failing to develop higher thinking skills. Both recommended greater exposure to liberal arts and sciences subjects, pointing out that established professions such as law and medicine saved technical training for graduate work in order to keep undergraduate liberal arts education intact.[12]

By the 1960s the early giants of accounting research (e.g., Hatfield, Sprague, Paton, Littleton, and Vatter) fell from academic favor. Absent from their work were both data and theory. Their work had focused on issues such as whether goodwill is an asset, whether to measure balances at cost or value, or whether an accounting unit should be considered a proprietorship or an entity.[13]

In 1960 the University of Chicago established the Center for Research in Security Prices (CRSP, pronounced "crisp") to measure common stock returns. The first machine-readable, historical stock price database was released by CRSP in 1964. By this time high-speed computing allowed economists to evaluate security price movement with statistical tools. In 1970 finance professor Eugene Fama presented theory and evidence suggesting stock prices reflect the combined knowledge of all buyers and sellers about a company's prospects.[14]

He reasoned financial markets react quickly to newly released, relevant information. Security prices impound this information as investors seek trading profits. Adjusting stock prices reflect more information than that held by any individual. Prices thus represent *unbiased* estimates of issuer prospects: stock prices are just as likely to be lower or higher compared to a theoretically perfect level. Fama's efficient markets hypothesis (EMH) suggests investors cannot consistently mint money trading securities in liquid capital markets.

Use of integral calculus, algebraic transformation, and words like *submartingale model* scared away common readers. Few controllers or audit partners in 1970 would have had the willingness and ability to work through Fama's reasoning. Yet all could have quickly understood that profit-seeking traders digest economic information pretty fast. The EMH represents the first of three great finance ideas presented in this book.

No academic or investment professional today believes financial markets are perfectly efficient, but most concede they are competitive. Witness the difficulty stock pickers face trying to beat market indexes consistently after deducting transaction costs. A seminal study of 115 mutual funds over the period 1945 to 1964 found that on average mutual fund managers could not predict security prices and that there was little evidence any individual fund manager was able to achieve better results than expected from mere chance.[15] By 1972 accounting and finance researchers had accepted the usefulness of the EMH.[16]

In 1968 an article by Ray Ball and Philip Brown, "An Empirical Evaluation of Accounting Income Numbers," was published in the *Journal of Accounting Research*, a publication affiliated with the University of Chicago. The authors noted diversity of corporate accounting practice and wondered if net income figures were meaningful in light of their heterogeneity. These two reasoned that if net income is important to investors, stock prices should react to earnings announcements.

Using regression analysis, Ball and Brown compared income figures on Standard & Poor's Compustat tapes for the period 1946 through 1966 with contemporaneous stock price data maintained by CRSP. Analysis showed that when annual income figures differed from expected values, stock prices reacted in the same direction as the variance. Earnings thus have considerable information content, as evidenced by subsequent stock price movements.[17]

The article shifted academic accounting's center of gravity 120 miles north from Champaign to Hyde Park. The University of Illinois had produced the first PhD program in accounting, five presidents of the American Accounting Association, and well-known teachers such as A. C. Littleton, Robert Mautz, Norton Bedford, and Arthur Wyatt.

Chicago challenged this supremacy, nurturing economists such as William Beaver, Michael Jensen, Shyam Sunder, and George Benston, who used statistical inference to validate or disprove quantitative hypotheses. Their work focused on relationships between accounting information and security prices, moving accounting from a normative language to more of a positive science.

An early leader was Bill Beaver. Born in Peoria, near A. C.

Littleton's home of Bloomington, Beaver fast-tracked his way through Notre Dame and the University of Chicago's MBA and PhD programs. George Sorter served as his dissertation adviser. Beaver evaluated accounting ratios as predictors of business failure.

This work led Beaver to embrace the *event study*, where researchers evaluate stock or bond price reactions to discrete events such as merger announcements, stock splits, dividend increases, or, as Beaver did, accounting principle changes. Security price movements relative to those of the overall market allowed accounting researchers to assess the presence or absence of information content in accounting numbers.[18]

Beaver and his colleagues validated significant correlation between changes in reported earnings and stock prices. However, the relationship was not simple. Price movements often precede earnings releases, suggesting that information other than earnings (e.g., news of labor strikes, changing commodity prices, competitor entry) also affects stock prices. Isolating the effects of accounting disclosures on security prices from other noise proved difficult.

Chicago researchers, using numbers to test hypotheses quantitatively, gained academic clout over more qualitative colleagues. PhD dissertations became increasingly mathematical and abstract. Net income balances and security prices provided limitless data to be measured, and academics adjusted research to use available tools. One professor cited a metaphor of a person so busy polishing his glasses he didn't put them on in order to see.[19]

Another observer contrasted attendance at accounting conferences held at the University of Chicago in 1966 and 1982. Presenters at the earlier conference included a representative of the AICPA plus accounting and finance executives. The latter conference was composed entirely of academics. Accounting research gained academic respectability but became more removed from practice.[20] Increasingly, sophisticated research became tough sledding for a practitioner who had taken a year of calculus plus an introductory statistics course.

Some Chicago-trained PhDs moved to the University of Rochester to form the positive school of accounting research under Ross Watts and Jerold Zimmerman. These two attempted to explain and predict accounting practices instead of making value judgments about their selection. They asked, for example, why steel companies switched from accelerated depreciation to straight-line in 1968.

The positive school sought structural explanations for management choices about accounting practices. Statistical research showed that greater use of debt financing was correlated with accounting selections that boost the present value of reported earnings. The likely causal relationship is that debt-laden firms have incentives to avoid violating accounting covenants in borrowing agreements. Correlation, however, does not prove causation.

The researchers also found that managers with earnings-based compensation schemes choose accounting methods that increase reported earnings and that larger firms, presumably subject to greater regulatory scrutiny, choose accounting methods that depress reported earnings. This analysis did not try to answer normative questions of whether these behaviors were good or bad.

An implication of the EMH and related statistical research was that financial accounting standards do not matter. Investors in aggregate review all sorts of accounting and nonaccounting data to divine company prospects. As shown with the LIFO controversy, there is considerable evidence that investors see through accounting form. Well-functioning capital markets may not need strict conformance with clearly articulated financial accounting rules. If investors were indeed slaves to accounting income, a few bright analysts could earn enormous trading profits after making adjustments for cosmetic accounting standards and policies. No one has yet found a way to do this.

Practitioner and regulator reaction to scientific analysis was lukewarm. Some felt academics were too busy running regressions to pay attention to the real world. Sandy Burton, SEC chief accountant, opined in a 1975 speech that accounting models had grown up in practice over many years based on common sense. Accounting lacks measurement purity but has the benefit of being understood. Economic models, by contrast, were never burdened by needs for practical record keeping.[21]

Writing in 1983, General Motors' deputy assistant controller felt there was growing recognition by the FASB and SEC that stock markets can process information for major publicly traded companies.[22] However, this recognition did not change the behavior of either organization.

Arthur Wyatt, chief technical accounting partner at Arthur Andersen & Co. and former University of Illinois accounting professor, also wrote in 1983, before joining the FASB, "few accountants in practice are aware of the [EMH] concept and a lot fewer understand it."[23]

He had seen clients forgo tax savings to report higher earnings under FIFO (covered in Chapter 3), enter into hedging transactions to mitigate accounting risk from foreign currency translation volatility (discussed later in Chapter 9), jump through hoops to structure acquisitions as pooling of interests (Chapter 10), and accept expensive financing terms to keep debt off balance sheets (Chapter 11). In short, Wyatt's experience was that corporate managers acted as if the stock market is *not* efficient. Accounting professionals, he believed, either ignored or disputed the validity of EMH and of underlying research.

An efficient stock market should prevent errant accounting behavior. One would think that doing dumb things to finesse earnings would depress a firm's stock price and get its executives fired. However, the EMH may not be sufficient to discipline these managers if they hold incorrect beliefs about investor behavior.[24] *Sure, I understand cash flow trumps accounting earnings, but those naive investors do not; I'll make accounting choices that give them earnings trajectories they think they want.*

➤

Critics of CAP and the APB had charged that these bodies had promulgated financial accounting standards in the absence of guiding principles. Bulletins and Opinions represented ad hoc fixes while academic attempts to fashion accounting postulates gathered dust.

The FASB sought a foundation to support its Statements. The resulting Conceptual Framework became the largest, most expensive effort ever undertaken to document a theory of financial reporting. The seven Statements of Financial Accounting Concepts published over 22 years consumed untold millions of dollars and man-hours to produce.

At the time of this writing, the Conceptual Framework stands as the reigning champion of accounting theory. This work represents the best effort put forth by standard setters to craft a science of accounting. The Framework does not codify accounting rules, a task that has proved impossible to date. Instead, the Framework offers principles the FASB has increasingly used to frame financial accounting debate.

Table 7.1 is an attempt to condense 200 pages of text to one chart.

Statement of Financial Accounting Concepts (SFAC) 1 has roots with the Trueblood Report. Financial statements should provide information allowing external parties to assess the amount, timing, and certainty of a corporation's future cash flows. Paragraph 50's discussion of management's stewardship responsibility addresses agency problems cited by Jensen and Meckling. The next paragraph's discussion of earning power reflects thinking embodied in Graham and Dodd's classic investment primer.

Qualities of accounting information are ranked by SFAC 2. At the top of the heap are *relevance* (information that makes a difference) and *reliability* (information that can be verified). Anecdotal evidence suggests that financial statement users prefer

Table 7.1   Conceptual Framework's Statements of Financial Accounting Concepts

	Issued	Title	Summary Point
1	Nov. 1978	*Objectives of Financial Reporting by Business Enterprises*	Financial accounting allows outsiders to assess the amount, timing, and certainty of a firm's future cash flows.
2	May 1980	*Qualitative Characteristics of Accounting Information*	Accounting's usefulness for decision making requires reported balances to be relevant and reliable.
3	Dec. 1980	*Elements of Financial Statements of Business Enterprises*	Superseded by Concept Statement 6.
4	Dec. 1980	*Objectives of Financial Reporting by Nonbusiness Organizations*	Nonprofits do not have simple performance measures or ownership interests that can be sold or transferred.
5	Dec. 1984	*Recognition and Measurement in Financial Statements of Business Enterprises*	Recognition requires measurability, relevance, and reliability. Measurement methods: historical and current costs, plus market, realizable, and present values.
6	Dec. 1985	*Elements of Financial Statements*	Defines assets, liabilities, equity, comprehensive income, revenues, expenses, gains, and losses, plus investments by and distributions to owners.
7	Feb. 2000	*Using Cash Flow Information and Present Value in Accounting Measurements*	Provides framework for using cash flow and present value tools in accounting measurement.

relevant, soft information while auditors favor the rigor of easily verified balances. Chapter 8 shows how the FASB abandoned inflation accounting standards because evidence suggested outsiders did not consider reported balances to be relevant.

In SFAC 5, guidance on what information should be incorporated in financial statements and when balances should be recognized is provided. Paragraph 9 bluntly states that recognition means depiction of an item in both words and numbers in the body of the financial statements. Footnote or other supplemental disclosures do not constitute accounting recognition. The FASB gives little credence to findings of Ball, Brown, Beaver, and others that capital markets impound all available information to set unbiased security prices. In other words, the FASB appears to reject the EMH.[25]

Representing the guts of the project, SFAC 6 presents definitions for 10 building blocks of financial statements. The major idea is definition of comprehensive income: the change in equity during a period from events and transactions from nonowner sources. Reporting comprehensive income means companies must figure unrealized gains and losses on unsettled transactions such as foreign currency translation adjustments and passive equity investments.

Companies report accumulated other comprehensive income as a component of shareholders' equity. By including both realized and unrealized transactions in the equity account, the FASB shifted financial statement emphasis from the income statement back to the balance sheet. The balance sheet had been supreme in the age of railroads, lost its luster with the rise of equities, and made a comeback thanks to the Conceptual Framework.

Balance sheet primacy perhaps better ties rules to the double-entry identity of assets equaling the sum of liabilities plus shareholders' equity. Standard setters and auditors may prefer balance sheet focus because it is easier to count stock values at a given date than flows over a time period.

Statements by the FASB on income taxes, investments, foreign currency, and pensions, described in subsequent chapters, illustrate the balance sheet's renaissance in standard setting. Financial statement users and the financial media, however, remain rooted in net income numbers based on realized transactions. Time will tell if the investing public follows the FASB's lead in placing primacy once again on the balance sheet.

At the end of the day, a humble accountant must decide whether to recognize a transaction in an accounting period, what dollar amount to assign to that item, and where in the financial statements the item should appear. Economic research has helped predict how accounting practices affect security prices, but this science has yet to tell a bookkeeper what to do.

8

INFLATION

The issue of inflation accounting is the first instance where academics were able to apply science to resolve a financial accounting debate. This chapter serves as a case study of what could happen if academics and practitioners communicate more effectively.

Accounting requires a common unit of measure. In 1792 the United States affirmed the dollar as its monetary unit, the first time a modern country selected a decimal currency system.[1] However, with the exception of Continental notes printed during the Revolutionary War (hence the phrase "not worth a Continental"), the early federal government did not issue currency.

Instead, banks printed paper demand notes. In theory depositors could redeem certificates at issuing banks for gold or silver.

By 1860 thousands of bank notes circulated in the U.S. economy and creditworthiness varied by issuer. The absence of a uniform definition of a dollar casts doubt on the reliability of contemporaneous financial records. The Union government enacted Civil War legislation to create nationally chartered banks that could issue demand notes backed by government securities. Dollar-based accounts gained meaning.

In 1913, the year modern income taxation became law, the government created the Federal Reserve System to serve as a central bank and promote monetary stability. The System received authority to issue the Federal Reserve notes that became America's uniform currency. However, a dollar's purchasing power still varied with changing prices.

Since the 1930s American accounting viewed the number of dollars used to acquire an asset as the basis for balance sheet valuation. Historical cost allowed accountants and auditors to look up actual prices paid. Revaluation after acquisition becomes problematic because subsequent values may not be reliable.

Inflation strains historical costs' usefulness. Sustained price inflation erodes a currency's purchasing power and forces buyers to use more dollars to buy a given asset. Long-held assets like land may be carried on balance sheets at fractions of replacement cost. Early LIFO adopters still have inventory valued at costs prevailing during World War II.

Further complication comes from inflation's uneven nature. Some goods like consumer electronics have experienced consistently falling prices, while replacement costs for labor-intensive services like masonry or woodworking have soared. No simple factor restates all assets into a meaningful level of purchasing power. Another complication is that price and quantity measures do not reflect improving quality. A passenger car's price today exceeds the number of dollars required to purchase a car 15 years earlier, but the higher purchase price is due in part to better technology and engineering.

Most significantly, inflation may cause mismatching. Revenues reflect prices at time of sale, while expenses reflect historical machining and inventory costs. Old costs matched with today's prices may bring illusory profit, mere holding gain from the run-up of market prices of inventory or plant and equipment.

Although margins appear strong, firms reporting mismatched profits must spend considerably more money to replace the inventory or equipment consumed. Taxable income calculated from outdated cost of goods sold or depreciation figures creates outsized liabilities and confiscates owners' capital. Executive compensation plans based on accounting earnings could reward managers for little more than realizing holding gains. Ill-informed managers could even distribute dividends from illusory profits and deplete a firm's productive capacity.

As a stylized example, suppose a common carrier spent $100,000 in 1979 to buy a truck with a five-year estimated useful life. Using straight-line depreciation based on historical cost, the firm charged $20,000 in annual depreciation. Revenue growth came from 5 percent annual rate increases tied to general inflation. Assume truck replacement costs grew three times as fast as general inflation. Table 8.1 summarizes these facts.

By simply raising prices 5 percent per year, the firm showed steadily increasing profit because reported depreciation failed to reflect surging replacement costs. Cost inflation and a generous 40 percent dividend payout depleted productive capacity.

On a replacement cost basis the firm should have charged $23,000 of depreciation in 1980 ($20,000 × 1.15), $26,500 in 1981 ($23,000 × 1.15), and so on. Historical cost accounting understated depreciation and overstated income. Holding gains should not have been distributed to owners through dividends. Distributions represent forgone reinvestment. Because dividends depended on reported earnings, which were overstated due to insufficient depreciation charges, the company depleted capital beginning in 1981. Excessive dividends hurt employees, suppliers, and creditors.

➤

Table 8.1   Inflation Can Bring Illusory Profits and Capital Erosion

	1979	1980	1981	1982	1983
Revenues (000s) [+ 5% per year]	$100.0	$105.0	$110.3	$115.8	$121.6
Operating expenses [+5%]	(70.0)	(73.5)	(77.2)	(81.0)	(85.1)
Recorded depreciation	(20.0)	(20.0)	(20.0)	(20.0)	(20.0)
Pretax income	10.0	11.5	13.1	14.8	16.5
Income taxes at 35%	(3.5)	(4.0)	(4.6)	(5.2)	(5.8)
Net income	6.5	7.5	8.5	9.6	10.7
Dividend payout at 40%	(2.6)	(3.0)	(3.4)	(3.8)	(4.3)
Reinvested earnings	$ 3.9	$ 4.5	$ 5.1	$ 5.8	$ 6.4
Reported revenues	$100.0	$105.0	$110.3	$115.8	$121.6
Reported operating expenses	(70.0)	(73.5)	(77.2)	(81.0)	(85.1)
Adjusted depreciation [+15%]	(20.0)	(23.0)	(26.5)	(30.4)	(35.0)
Pro forma pretax income	10.0	8.5	6.6	4.4	1.5
Actual income taxes	(3.5)	(4.0)	(4.6)	(5.2)	(5.8)
Pro forma net income (loss)	6.5	4.5	2.0	(0.8)	(4.3)
Actual dividends	(2.6)	(3.0)	(3.4)	(3.8)	(4.3)
Pro forma reinvested earnings	$ 3.9	$ 1.5	$ (1.4)	$ (4.6)	$ (8.6)

Theorists had discussed inflation's effects on financial reporting since the early 1900s. In the 1920s, William Paton wrote about the unstable, variable nature of a dollar as a unit of measure. Arthur Andersen & Co.'s Leonard Spacek, the critic of the Committee on Accounting Procedure (CAP), advocated depreciation charges based on asset replacement costs.

Except for the 1939 tax rule to permit LIFO for financial reporting and tax accounting, standard setters made no meaningful changes to reporting standards. In December 1947, CAP issued Bulletin 33, *Depreciation and High Costs*, to document consideration given "to the problem of making adequate provision for the replacement of plant facilities in view of recent sharp increases in the price level." The Committee rejected any requirement to restate fixed asset values from concern there would be no objective standard to judge the propriety of restated depreciation charges.

Two methods subsequently emerged to restate nominal dollar balances. *Constant dollar* accounting uses a general price level index to express historical balances in terms of a consistent measure of purchasing power. The U.S. consumer price index and gross national product (GNP) deflator were recommended indexes. *Current cost* accounting attempts to measure prevailing replacement costs of some portion of a firm's productive capacity. Replacement cost measures sector-specific adjustments to reflect inflation's uneven nature across an economy.

Inflation receded between the Korean and Vietnam wars. The Accounting Research Division, sister organization the Accounting Principles Board, issued Accounting Research Study 6 in 1963. *Reporting the Financial Effects of Price-Level Changes* advocated restated financial statements showing effects of general price level adjustments. Few paid attention to the monograph.

The APB issued Statement 3, *Financial Statements Restated for General Price-Level Changes*, in June 1969. APB Statements did not require specific disclosures and carried less weight than the APB's more formal Opinions. Statement 3 recommended publication of supplemental price-level adjustments using the Commerce Department's quarterly GNP deflator and opined that comprehensive restatement of complete financial statements was the only way to help users adjust for general price-level changes on an informed basis.

Even though all 18 members of the 1969 APB supported Statement 3, it had no effect on American financial reporting practices. One public company, the Indiana Telephone Corporation, followed the Statement's recommendation.[2]

In October 1973, conflict erupted between Arabs and Israelis in what became known as the Yom Kippur War. A subsequent Arab oil embargo led to a quadrupling of oil prices and renewed price inflation. In 1974 the FASB issued a Discussion Memorandum and then an Exposure Draft. *Financial Reporting in Units of General Purchasing Power* recommended use of constant dollar accounting and adjustments based on a general price index.

Congress vests the SEC with authority to promulgate U.S. financial accounting standards. The SEC had informally delegated standard setting to the CAP and APB. If it chose, the SEC could issue its own standards for publicly traded companies. Accounting treatment for the investment tax credit (ITC) and oil and gas exploration were notable examples. In the mid-1970s, the SEC's chief accountant, John Burton, chose to exercise this authority.

Brash, brainy Sandy Burton, son of a CPA, served as a statistician for the Brooklyn Dodgers while a college student. After graduating from Haverford College, a liberal arts school that doesn't teach accounting, he enrolled in Columbia's MBA program and then joined Arthur Young & Company's audit staff. He left public accounting to earn a doctorate from Columbia and signed on to its business school faculty. In 1972 he was appointed SEC chief accountant, serving five years before becoming New York City's Deputy Mayor for Finance during the city's financial crisis. In the 1980s he returned to Columbia Business School to serve as dean.

Burton demonstrated his attention to detail by delivering a 6,000-word speech that dissected the phrase *presents fairly* in the context of an auditor's report[3]—an exegesis that would have made any biblical scholar proud. The chief accountant became interested in inflation's effect on historical cost financial statements and concluded that sector-specific replacement costs better suit the needs of financial statement users. He pressed the point through comments and speeches.

He derided the simpler approach of adjusting historical costs on the basis of a general inflation index. Burton twisted the FASB term *purchasing power units* to create the acronym PuPU and express disdain for mechanistic adjustment based on a single price index.[4] The disproportionate increase in oil prices supported Burton's argument that specific costs were more relevant to an enterprise than general inflation as measured by a broad index.

Jawboning by the SEC influenced the FASB's November 1975 decision to defer issuance of an inflation accounting statement. Instead, the FASB spent the next three years studying inflation accounting and the experiences of 101 companies participating in a field test of the 1974 Exposure Draft.

In March 1976 the SEC issued Accounting Series Release 190, *Notice of Adoption of Amendments to Regulation S-X Requiring Disclosure of Certain Replacement Cost Data.* ASR 190 required registrants with inventories and fixed assets greater than $100 million to file supplementary balance sheet replacement cost data as well as restated cost of goods sold and depreciation figures in the annual Form 10-K. Critics charged that this directive threatened to introduce greater inconsistency in financial reporting practices.

Finally, in September 1979, just before the United States was to feel the effects of the second oil shock resulting from the Iranian Revolution and hostage crisis, the FASB issued Statement 33, *Financial Reporting and Changing Prices,* to address the perceived urgent need for providing inflation disclosures.

Statement 33 took notice of SEC preferences and required both current cost and constant purchasing power estimates for inventory and fixed assets in a supplementary statement. The FASB stated that if the SEC did not rescind ASR 190 when Statement 33 became effective, the Board would make necessary amendments to Statement 33 requirements and deadlines. The SEC subsequently relented and phased out requirements of ASR 190.[5]

In describing Statement 33 as an experiment and inserting a sunset clause, the FASB explained:

> Preparers and users of financial reports have not yet reached a consensus on the general, practical usefulness of constant dollar and current cost information. It seems unlikely that a consensus can be

reached until further experience has been gained with the use of both types of information in systematic practical applications. . . . The Board makes no pretense of having solved all of the implementation problems.[6]

Statement 33 requirements extended for a five-year period at the end of which its merits would be evaluated. Success meant both users and preparers deemed disclosures useful. The Statement applied to companies with inventories and property, plant, and equipment of more than $125 million or total assets of more than $1 billion. Ironically, both the SEC and FASB used nominal dollar balances to set the scope for compliance with inflation accounting rules.

The recommended constant dollar index was the Bureau of Labor Statistics' monthly consumer price index, not the Commerce Department's quarterly GNP deflator. There was no requirement to issue a complete inflation-adjusted balance sheet or income statement. In defense of constant dollar accounting, the FASB cited preferences of statement preparers and auditors. I believe this preference stemmed from auditors' aversion to exercising judgment and resulting litigation exposure.

Just weeks after issuance of Statement 33, the University of Chicago's Sid Davidson, one of the 18 members of the 1969 APB that had promulgated Statement 3, predicted that a great number of the estimated 1,300 firms affected would report having declared dividends in excess of income from continuing operations. Inflation accounting would mark a breakthrough in financial reporting.[7]

Instead, the business community greeted Statement 33 with a yawn. Economic studies found little stock market reaction to inflation disclosures from either ASR 190 or Statement 33. In the parlance of academia, inflation-adjusted data did not appear to provide *value-relevant* information. In November 1984, the FASB issued Statement 82, which eliminated the need for general price level disclosure.

Personal experience supports these academic findings. In early 1985 I audited the inflation footnote of International Paper Company's 1984 annual report. After wading through exhausting chains of calculations to restate plant values, I questioned management about fluctuations in restated figures. It became obvious the client did not use these figures to make operating or investment decisions.

"After five years of experimenting with inflation-adjusted accounting, most of corporate America ranks it about 57th on the burning-issue list—somewhere after the danger of invasion by crazed Canadian geese,"[8] began a November 1985 *Forbes* article. The author quoted a DuPont executive who commented that while his company could estimate what it would cost to replace a nylon plant, the exercise would not be relevant because the company would simply upgrade the facility's capabilities.

An outlying advocate of inflation accounting cited in the article was FMC Corporation (formerly Food Machinery Corporation), a diversified manufacturer requiring managers to use inflation-adjusted numbers for internal reporting and decision making. The company's sophisticated management reporting system motivated me to interview for a position on its finance staff when I was in business school in 1986.

FMC's stock price had soared from a leveraged recapitalization. Subsequent operations did not bring commensurate growth in market capitalization. A personal learning was that a sophisticated management reporting system is not a sufficient condition for sustained wealth creation.

In December 1986, the FASB threw in the towel and issued Statement 89. Firms were encouraged but not required to disclose current cost inflation information. The Statement provided guidelines for inflation-adjusted disclosures and encouraged experimentation.

Three of the seven FASB members dissented with Statement 89. David Mosso believed that "accounting for the interrelated effects of general and specific price changes is the most critical set of issues that the Board will face"⁹ in the twentieth century. Even though inflation rates had moderated by the late 1980s, inflation's compound effect through time remains substantial.

The 2004 *Accounting Trends & Techniques* survey of accounting practices followed by 600 public corporations did not show any firm making voluntary current cost restatements of inventories or fixed assets.[10] At the beginning of the twenty-first century, inflation accounting was a dead issue.

Figure 8.1 presents an inflation time series based on year-over-year changes in consumer prices since 1914. Inflation spiked at the end of the World Wars and Korean War and then remained modest until the 1970s. During this quiet period, accounting practitioners ignored suggestions made by the AICPA's Accounting Research

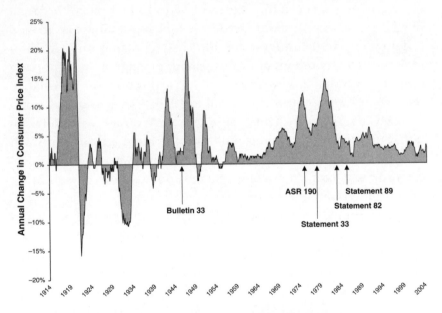

**Figure 8.1   Inflation Accounting Standards
Reacted to Environmental Change**
Source: Computed from Bureau of Labor Statistics' Consumer Price Index, All Urban Consumers.

Division and people like Arthur Andersen's Leonard Spacek, evidence that financial accounting needs a crisis to spur standard setting.

Bulletin 33 came after the wave of post–World War II inflation, and ASR 190 came on the heels of the first oil shock. Statement 89, which killed off inflation accounting, came with decelerating inflation. A literature search showed that tame inflation in the 1990s corresponded with an absence of discussion on this topic in the business press.

Tactically, the inflation accounting experiment failed. Users did not find restated balances relevant or reliable. In addition, LIFO inventory accounting provided only a partial solution because inventory costs remaining on the balance sheet became increasingly out of date. Strategically, the debate showed that academics could help statement preparers resolve a financial accounting dispute.

Another silver cloud, opined one observer, was that Statement 33 disclosures spurred passage of the corporation-friendly 1981 Economic Recovery Tax Act that provided for faster depreciation rates, and earlier deductions, on corporate tax returns.[11] This case study also shows that science can be used to evaluate financial accounting standards.

9

VOLATILITY

Markets may be efficient but they still hate two things, volatility and surprises.

—Jerome York, former CFO of Chrysler and IBM,
Fortune, November 24, 1997

The second seminal event in the history of corporate finance was development of the capital asset pricing model (CAPM). Financial statement preparers, however, paid little attention to this groundbreaking concept. Corporate management consequently did not overcome an ill-conceived fear of reporting volatile earnings.

In 1960, 26-year-old UCLA economics PhD candidate William Sharpe needed a dissertation topic. While also working at the nearby RAND Corporation, Sharpe met economist Harry Markowitz.[1]

Markowitz's famous 1952 paper "Portfolio Selection" studied risk and return for collections of financial assets. He showed that diversification reduces risk. However, Markowitz struggled to pinpoint how correlation among returns of individual holdings influences aggregate portfolio risk.

Discussions between the two suggested a dissertation topic on security prices and required returns of financial assets held in a portfolio. Required return, also known as cost of equity, represents expected earnings needed to attract equity capital for a particular investment.[2] This forward-looking measure depends on investor sentiment and cannot be observed directly.

Sharpe attacked the problem and presented findings at the University of Chicago in 1962. Reactions were so favorable he received a job offer, which he declined. Sharpe then submitted a summary paper to the prestigious *Journal of Finance*. The editor rejected the article.

Sharpe asked a referee to reevaluate the submission, and the journal subsequently published "Capital Asset Prices: A Theory of Market Equilibrium under Conditions of Risk" in September 1964. Chicago's Eugene Fama dubbed the work the CAPM. In 1990 Sharpe, Markowitz, and Merton Miller shared a Nobel Prize for laying the foundation of modern financial economics. Every college-level finance textbook today discusses Sharpe's model.

Sharpe argued that investment risk of a given stock is not about raw volatility. Investors face risks that can and cannot be eliminated through diversification. Buyers of financial instruments demand to be compensated for *systematic* risk resulting from swings in economic activity. They are less concerned with idiosyncratic risks specific to individual companies. Holding securities in a diversified portfolio mitigates the second exposure.

A major hurricane could cause substantial damage to homes in Miami. A local property insurer faces ruin. Financial markets will not punish this firm with exorbitant equity costs. Potential investors can diversify by holding shares in a lumber company that would see sales soar in the event of a major windstorm. The presence or absence of a hurricane would little influence combined returns of both securities.

Systematic risk, however, cannot be eliminated through

holding a diversified portfolio. Investors demand compensation for risk that varies with stock or bond markets as a whole. Firms with cyclical sales, high fixed costs, or lots of debt bear more systematic risk and endure higher capital costs. Since gold prices do not move with general economic activity, CAPM suggests a gold mine's capital costs would be low. A debt-laden, fixed-cost, cyclical telecom firm would have to offer robust returns to attract investors.

A startling implication of CAPM is that investors shrug off many corporate blips and hiccups. Earnings volatility associated with weather, litigation, and currency risks need not influence a firm's cost of equity and stock price. Supporting evidence comes from experiences of reinsurance companies. These firms assume enormous underwriting risks that ceding companies feel uncomfortable retaining. Although reinsurers can face extremely volatile earnings, they have traditionally had little trouble raising equity capital.

How does earnings volatility affect a firm's cost of equity? It's not clear. Economists have spilled much ink trying to isolate earnings patterns from other traits to measure equity financing costs. Numerous event studies suggest markets see through reported earnings. Yet there is evidence stock markets react unfavorably to events that increase accounting volatility even in the absence of increased economic exposure.[3] No academic has disproved Jerome York, quoted at the beginning of the chapter.

Financial accounting's purpose is to help outsiders project the amount, timing, and certainty of a firm's future cash flows. Problems with reporting volatility have caused tension between standard setters and statement preparers since the 1930s. Managers believe investors consider bumpy earnings a blemish when evaluating a firm's earning power: reporting smooth, predictable earnings will boost a company's stock price. By contrast, standard setters want companies to tell it like it is, alerting outsiders to the presence of warts on a corporate earnings trajectory.

Three case studies illustrate this tension. The first concerns foreign currency translation. Countries designate currencies as the local medium of exchange. The U.S. dollar's market price relative to another currency depends on supply and demand factors arising from political and economic events.

U.S. firms seeking to buy goods or services in Britain typically first exchange dollars for pounds. The number of dollars required to acquire the necessary number of pounds depends on the currency's exchange rate. If a U.S. firm sells goods or services using pounds, then it must convert the foreign currency back to dollars before bringing profits home, a process known as repatriation.

Exchange rates vary between transaction and repatriation dates. Foreign currency translation seeks to express transactions as if they had been initially recorded in the parent company's currency. The problem is that many transactions remain open when the firm issues financial statements.

Foreign currency translation uses interim exchange rates to record consequences of incomplete transactions (i.e., activity in progress before cash is returned to the home country). Repatriation comes through intercompany dividend payments or proceeds from the sale or liquidation of a foreign operation. Periodic reporting requires selection of interim exchange rates and classification of the balancing figure arising from the translation process.

Accountants generally select among three exchange rates in this process: the historical rate in effect when a transaction began, the current rate as of the most recent balance sheet date, or an average rate for balances flowing through an income statement. The so-called plug figure to balance accounts was generally charged or credited to shareholders' equity on the balance sheet.

As an illustrative example, suppose a U.S. firm established a British subsidiary when the exchange rate was $1.50 per pound. The pound gradually appreciated to $2.00 as of the balance sheet date. One attempt to convert foreign financial statement balances from pounds to dollars appears in Table 9.1.

**Table 9.1 Currency Translation Adjustment
Keeps Financial Statements Balanced**

	Local Currency	Translation Basis	Exchange Rate	Home Currency
Income Statement				
Revenues	£200,000	Average	1.90	$380,000
Cost of goods sold	(130,000)	Historical	1.85	(240,500)
Administrative expenses	(42,000)	Average	1.90	(79,800)
Interest expense	(8,000)	Average	1.90	(15,200)
Income before taxes	20,000			44,500
Income taxes	(7,000)	Average	1.90	(13,300)
Net income	£ 13,000			$ 31,200
Balance Sheet				
Cash	£ 5,000	Current	2.00	$ 10,000
Accounts receivable	25,000	Current	2.00	50,000
Inventory	40,000	Historical	1.90	76,000
Plant and equipment	100,000	Historical	1.80	180,000
Total assets	£170,000			$316,000
Accounts payable	£ 22,000	Current	2.00	44,000
Long-term debt	100,000	Current	2.00	200,000
Total liabilities	122,000			244,000
Common stock and paid-in capital	15,000	Historical	1.50	22,500
Beginning retained earnings	20,000	Historical	1.80	36,000
Current net income	13,000			31,200
Ending retained earnings	33,000			67,200
Translation adjustment (plug)	—			(17,700)
Shareholders' equity	48,000			72,000
Total liabilities and equity	£170,000			$316,000

This example translates monetary assets and liabilities with the exchange rate in effect as of the balance sheet date, nonmonetary items using historical rates in effect when the assets and liabilities were initially recorded, and income statement items other than depreciation using an average exchange rate for the year. Table 9.1 shows how use of three different rates means the balance sheet no longer balances.

The company borrowed £100,000 in debt to finance construction of plant and equipment when the exchange rate was $1.80. In dollar terms the firm acquired $180,000 of debt and a factory worth $180,000. After the pound appreciated to $2.00, the debt and factory (before depreciation) increased in value to $200,000. However, translating the nonmonetary factory with the historical exchange rate capped the factory's remeasurement at $180,000 and created an unfavorable $20,000 discrepancy.

Combined translation differences from use of varied rates required an unfavorable $17,700 adjustment to keep statements balanced. The adjustment had no effect on cash flows. It simply equated debits with credits. Which exchange rate (historical, average for the year, current) and what do with the translation adjustment represent the crux of the foreign currency accounting.

The 1944 Bretton Woods Agreement controlled currency exchange rates and limited foreign currency accounting's significance. Bulletin 4, issued by CAP in 1939, provided soft guidance on selection of exchange rates for translation of financial statement balances. The APB's Opinion 6, issued 1965, gave credence to translating long-term receivables and liabilities at current exchange rates. Otherwise, currency accounting remained a dormant issue.

Things changed on Sunday, August 15, 1971. President Richard Nixon imposed price and wage controls and closed the gold window, no longer allowing foreign central banks to exchange dollars for gold. Bretton Woods rules ceased to exist. Within two years the world economy moved to a system of floating exchange rates where market forces continually revise the dollar's value in other currencies.

In its waning months, the APB recognized the significance of fluctuating exchange rates but did not provide guidance. The first Statement of the newly formed FASB in December 1973 was to acknowledge the problem and require disclosure of translation policies (the "Translation Basis" column in Table 9.1) and disclosure of where the firm classified the adjustment in the financial statements (i.e., flowed through the income statement or posted directly to shareholders' equity).

In October 1975 the FASB pressed further and issued Statement 8, requiring the translation adjustment to be classified as an exchange gain or loss and included in income statements. Financial statement preparers revolted. Malcolm Forbes wrote an editorial decrying the standard.[4]

Currency market machinations could determine a company's income for the year and impair management's goal of reporting a smooth earnings trajectory. In our example, the Statement 8 translation adjustment would erase 40 percent of the subsidiary's translated pretax earnings even though cash flows remained unaffected.

Academics found that the only meaningful consequence of Statement 8 was that multinational firms embraced currency contracts designed to minimize fluctuation in noncash accounting adjustments. To avoid earnings volatility, corporations risked cash resources in forward exchange contracts to hedge noncash exposures[5] and smooth earnings trends.

In May 1978 the FASB requested constituent comments concerning its first 12 Statements. Eighty-five percent of comments received requested reconsideration of Statement 8.[6]

In December 1981 the FASB issued Statement 52, requiring self-contained subsidiaries to translate balance sheet figures at current rates (reducing the magnitude of balance-sheet-related currency adjustments) and to record the translation adjustment as a separate component of shareholders' equity. The FASB here showed early focus on the balance sheet and classifying open transactions as comprehensive income.

With issuance of Statement 52, reported earnings no longer bore consequences of volatile currency markets. Mollified management teams preparing statements were less concerned with fluctuations in shareholders' equity balances. Statement 52 moved currency translation off everyone's radar screen.

A second case study on earnings volatility comes from the influence of interest rates and stock returns on annual pension obligations. Defined benefit pensions sprouted after World War II to guarantee payments to retired workers based on annual wages and years of service at the company. Determining the annual cost of this promise requires rate projections for employee tenure, wages, life expectancy, and investment returns. Defined benefit pension accounting makes depreciation look like child's play.

What makes the liability so difficult to value is its long time horizon and resulting sensitivity to modest adjustments in discount rates and projected investment returns. Innocent changes in economic projections could erase or double a firm's annual pension expense.

At a high level, pension expense flowing through an income statement has three components:

Pension expense = Service cost + Interest cost − Portfolio returns

Service cost represents growth in pension liabilities from employees having worked an additional year. Interest cost means growth in the pension liability from the passage of time: with every year future payment obligations become due 12 months sooner. Portfolio returns comprise the income from and appreciation of invested assets to pay future benefits.

In November 1948 CAP issued Bulletin 36, the first pension accounting standard. Bulletin 36 required that accumulated unfunded service costs from previous years of employment (i.e., starting a plan and giving employees credit for years worked before plan creation) should be recognized over the remaining service life of employees. The rule would result in better matching, the Committee felt, because establishment of a pension produces future benefits such as better morale, removal of superannuated employees from the payroll, and attraction and retention of more desirable personnel.

Most sponsoring companies put money into trusts that assumed responsibility for investments and making future pension payments. Accountants recognized as pension expense the amount of cash that management chose to put into trusts in a given year.

In September 1956 CAP issued Bulletin 47 to encourage companies to recognize pension liabilities on balance sheets for unfunded balances that had *vested* (become earned by employees). An example of a purported financial reporting abuse was Swift & Company's decision to cut 1957 pension contributions to $1.1 million from $13.6 million the previous year. The discretionary difference accounted for almost all of Swift's reported 1957 profits. Arthur Young & Company, after backstage debate, gave its audit client a clean opinion.

In November 1966 the APB's 20 members unanimously adopted Opinion 8, *Accounting for the Cost of Pension Plans*, which required a formal accrual process for matching all current and future compensation costs with revenues earned in a period. Opinion 11 on tax accounting, issued 13 months later, represented the apex of matching in U.S. financial accounting standards. Some commentators feel Opinion 8 represented a successful standard because the APB used a formal research study in the deliberation process and reduced diversity of accounting practice.[7]

Opinion 8 marked a turning point in standard setting. Since 1939 U.S. standard setters had offered broad guidance. Now the APB offered a detailed prescription for calculating pension expense. Consider paragraph 17b discussing the maximum permissible expense figure:

> The annual provision for pension cost should not be greater than the total of (1) normal cost, (2) 10 per cent of the past service cost

(until fully amortized), (3) 10 per cent of the amounts of any increases or decreases in prior service cost arising on amendments of the plan (until fully amortized) and (4) interest equivalents under paragraph 42 or 43 on the difference between provisions and amounts funded.

The passage reads more like tax return instructions than guidance for keeping a set of books. Price Waterhouse's Carl Tietjen described Opinion 8 as the beginning of financial accounting's cookbook era.[8]

Two constituents benefited from the replacement of a principle with a rule: the SEC received protection from charges of political favoritism, and auditors could reduce malpractice litigation by demonstrating company compliance with quantitative standards.[9] The loser was the role of judgment in the financial accounting profession.

The FASB tried to further narrow diversity of practice with a 1982 proposal that would have forced pension sponsors to recognize more debt on balance sheets. Economic studies had shown that investors already viewed unfunded obligations as liabilities, which raised borrowing costs and lowered issuer bond ratings. Forcing companies to recognize a greater pension liability, perhaps amounting to 9 percent of assets on the balance sheet, may not have provided additional, relevant information but would have caused borrowers to violate debt covenants.[10]

Five hundred comment letters, two rounds of public hearings, and five years of deliberation later, the FASB issued Statement 87, *Employers' Accounting for Pensions*, in December 1985, with three of the seven members dissenting. The standard narrowed the number of approved actuarial methods to calculate liabilities from five to one and expanded the definition of pension expense to include systematic amortization of prior service costs, actuarial gains and losses, and any transitional asset or liability arising from Statement adoption. An employer pension liability arises if funding falls below annual pension expense.

Credit markets determine interest rates and thus the discount rate required to calculate pensions' annual interest cost. Interest rates and stock returns also influence investment performance relative to changes in pension obligations. These volatile inputs together with the long-term nature of pension assets and liabilities create the likelihood of reporting volatile pension expense as real-world results diverge from plan assumptions.

Statement 87 did more to allow smoothing of earnings than any other U.S. accounting standard. The FASB permitted statement preparers to spread changes in investment projections and actuarial gains and losses over many years and to use the "accumulated other comprehensive income" section of shareholders' equity as a holding tank so that adjustments did not flow through the income statement.

There is compelling evidence that companies continued to change interest rate and investment returns assumptions to modify pension expense and further smooth reported earnings.[11]

A third case study comes from valuation of financial securities held in corporate portfolios. States govern U.S. corporation law. In 1889 New Jersey, domiciliary home of Standard Oil, allowed corporations to own stock of other companies.[12] Accountants soon struggled to reconcile historical cost accounting with the prevalence of market prices for liquid financial securities. It didn't seem logical to some that identical shares of a company purchased on different dates should be valued on the balance sheet at varied purchase prices.

Observable market prices seem to satisfy standard setters' tests of relevance and reliability. New York University's George Sorter quipped that if accounting statements can influence security prices, then why can't security prices affect accounting balances?

Use of historical cost invites trouble. Firms often hold securities purchased over time at wide-ranging costs. An opportunistic manager could sell appreciated securities in periods when the firm wanted to report more income. Such cherry-picking gives the appearance of steady earnings growth and saddles the firm with the remaining poorly performing securities.

Suppose a firm invested $1,000 in a liquid common stock and the position appreciated to $1,400 by the balance sheet date. How should the firm account for the investment when closing the books? Table 9.2 suggests three possibilities.

Method 1 presents the simplest solution: ignore changes in market values until the security is sold. After completing a sales transaction, the company records a gain or loss on the income statement for the difference between the market price and the carrying cost. In this example, no sale has taken place and no revaluation is recognized in the financial statements.

Method 2 adjusts the investment to the $1,400 market value, even though the security remains unsold. The mark-to-market adjustment creates an unrealized holding gain, raising pretax income by $400. The tax payment on the gain will not be due until the firm sells the security and collects cash, the realization principle discussed in Chapter 3. Consequently, the firm posts the future obligation as a deferred tax liability on the balance sheet.

Method 3 also marks the security to market, but the gain bypasses the income statement and is posted net of the deferred tax liability to accumulated other comprehensive income, the same holding tank used to record a running total of open-ended foreign currency translation and pension accounting adjustments.

Balance sheet totals are identical under Methods 2 and 3. Both methods mark the security to market, increase shareholders' equity by $260, and create a $140 deferred tax liability ($400 gain × 35 percent tax rate). Method 2 shows higher net income and retained earnings, while Method 3 quarantines the unrealized gain in accumulated other comprehensive income until management sells the security. Eventually, all three methods show the same cumulative results.

The first accounting standard to address so-called *fair value accounting* was Bulletin 30, issued by CAP in August 1947. Concerned

**Table 9.2   Three Ways to Account
for an Appreciated Equity Investment**

	Method 1	Method 2	Method 3
Income Statement			
Revenues	$1,782	$1,782	$1,782
Operating expenses	(1,475)	(1,475)	(1,475)
Operating income	307	307	307
Unrealized investment holding gain	0	400	0
Pretax income	307	707	307
Income taxes at 35%	(107)	(247)	(107)
Net income	$ 200	$ 460	$ 200
Balance Sheet			
Marketable securities	$1,000	$1,400	$1,400
Other assets	1,250	1,250	1,250
Total assets	$2,250	$2,650	$2,650
Deferred tax liability	$ 0	$ 140	$ 140
Other liabilities	1,025	1,025	1,025
Total liabilities	1,025	1,165	1,165
Common stock and paid-in capital	525	525	525
Beginning retained earnings	500	500	500
Current net income	200	460	200
Ending retained earnings	700	960	700
Accumulated other comprehensive income	0	0	260
Shareholders' equity	1,225	1,485	1,485
Total liabilities and equity	$2,250	$2,650	$2,650

with valuation of current assets and liabilities—assets to be realized and obligations to be satisfied within a year of the balance sheet date—the Committee felt that when the market value of a liquid security falls substantially below its cost and management considers the decline to be other than a temporary phenomenon, then carrying value should be written down to market value. Accountants shouldn't bother with normal security fluctuations.

Bulletin 30 extended the *lower of cost or market* rule used for inventory valuation to security holdings. Interestingly, one dissenting CAP member preferred that marketable securities be valued at market regardless of whether this amount was above or below cost.

In December 1975, the FASB issued Statement 12, *Accounting for Certain Marketable Equity Securities*, in reaction to the equity bear market of 1973–1974. The Statement addressed write-downs of common and preferred stock and did not consider what to do if equities appreciated from the original purchase price.

In lieu of tracking individual positions, Statement 12 required companies to use lower of cost or market accounting for baskets of stocks grouped into current and noncurrent portfolios. For the current portfolio, write-downs for aggregate market value declines, and write-ups up to purchase price for subsequent recoveries, would be included in the income statement consistent with Method 2 in Table 9.2. In the noncurrent portfolio, write-downs and write-ups should be recorded in a component of shareholders' equity consistent with Method 3.

Statement 12 was noticeably silent on bonds. Financial intermediaries typically invest more money in bonds than in stocks. New York City, a large issuer of municipal bonds, was nearly bankrupt. Large banks had made sizable loans to shaky foreign governments. And certain real estate developments, heavy users of debt financing, had failed. Statement 15, issued a year and a half later and mentioned in Chapter 6, addressed private loan restructuring, not valuation of publicly traded bonds.

Financial institutions continued to report debt securities at amortized cost. Yield-chasing investors, holding speculative bonds, could sell appreciated issues to recognize gains and keep depressed securities at cost in order to smooth reported earnings. The FASB understood the cherry-picking game.

The FASB's December 1991 Statement 107 required footnote disclosure of market values of financial instruments. Walther Schuetze, the SEC's chief accountant in 1992, advocated the mark-to-market accounting in financial statements even though market values were already disclosed in footnotes. He argued market values were more relevant for financial statement users and that retail investors used information published by investor services without footnotes. In this instance Schuetze clearly rejected the efficient markets hypothesis.[13]

In 1992 the FASB issued an exposed draft on valuing debt and equity securities at fair value. In the 90-day comment period it received comments from 600 respondents. Top of mind was the concern of reporting earnings volatility if financial securities were marked to market.

Learning from experience with foreign currency and pensions, the FASB issued Statement 115, *Accounting for Certain Investments in Debt and Equity Securities*, in May 1993. The statement created a middle ground to satisfy investors and management.

Statement 115 required use of three classifications of marketable securities. For debt securities that the company has both the intent and ability to hold to maturity, the company should carry them at amortized cost (Method 1). Absent default, holding gains and losses reverse by the time bonds mature.

Debt and equity securities bought and held for the purpose of selling them in the near future should be marked to market with the unrealized gains or losses posted to the income statement (Method 2).

Debt and equity securities not classified as either trading or held to maturity should be classified as available for sale. Under this approach, securities are also marked to market with the offsetting unrealized gains and losses posted to accumulated other comprehensive income in the balance sheet's shareholders' equity section (Method 3).

Companies have little latitude to change classification for designated securities. As a colleague noted, the FASB directed management to pick a lane and stay in it. Under Statement 115, held to maturity is a restrictive standard and leaves management little opportunity to sell a bond. Further, no company wants to subject reported income to the volatility of security markets. Almost all firms reject the trading classification. A notable exception was Enron, to be discussed in Chapter 14. By default, available for sale became the classification of choice for most organizations holding marketable securities.

Over the next decade, derivatives contracts (e.g., options, futures, forwards, and swaps) became increasingly popular investment and risk management tools. Standard setters sought fair market valuation of these financial contracts, while management sought to avoid reporting volatile earnings. In June 1998 the FASB issued Statement 133, the *War and Peace* of accounting standards.

Cutting through hundreds of pages of rules and interpretation, the Statement basically says that derivatives contracts represent assets and liabilities that must be shown on the balance sheet at fair market value. Changes in values of certain qualifying contracts may be accumulated in shareholders' equity and not flowed through the income statement. The FASB used the accumulated other comprehensive income account to pacify skittish managers.

Instead of accepting volatility as a normal consequence of business operations, Statement preparers embraced accumulated other comprehensive income as U.S. financial accounting's Island of Misfit Toys, a place to store unwanted volatility from mark-to-market accounting until a transaction was realized.

10

INTANGIBLES

*We are participating in a New Economy, and the rules have changed
dramatically. What you own is not as important as what you know.*

—1999 Enron Annual Report,
Letter to Shareholders

Financial accounting evolved from a means to monitor management stewardship of assets into a tool used by equity investors to value shares. Nowhere in this process did the field adapt to the rise of intangible assets. How to account for internally developed intangible assets remains the field's great unsolved mystery.

Intangible assets represent those invisible resources such as brand, culture, customer lists, and process knowledge that help companies grow profitably. These amorphous tools often cannot be bought or sold independently of the company itself. While managers must choose how to allocate scarce physical assets, employees can use intangible assets simultaneously in multiple locations. Many intangibles become more valuable with increased use.

In his 600-page book *Accounting Theory* written in 1970, Eldon Hendriksen devoted just 20 pages to intangible assets. Thirty years later, intangible resources came to be recognized as the only significant corporate asset class worth acquiring. Most receivables, inventory, machinery, and land can be replaced easily.

Creditor-based balance sheets put little emphasis on intangibles. Hard assets could be observed directly, sold in secondary markets, and used as collateral to secure loans. Intangibles offered lenders little comfort. As one commentator noted, if you can't kick it, how can you borrow against it?[1]

The time series shown in Figure 10.1 illustrates growing significance that equity investors placed on intangibles. Price-to-book ratio measures a company's market value divided by net assets on the balance sheet. A ratio of 1:1 means the stock market places the same value on a company's net assets as its accountants do. A ratio substantially above 1:1 indicates investors appraise net assets more enthusiastically than do financial accountants.

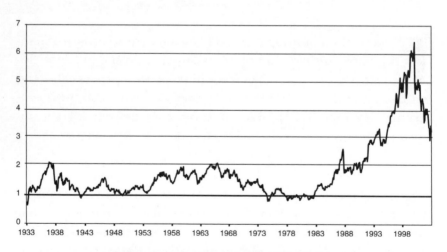

Figure 10.1   Price-to-Book Ratio of
Dow Jones Industrial Average: 1933 to 2002
Source: CashflowValuation.com

From the 1933 Securities Act until the mid-1980s, the price-to-book ratio for the 30 stocks in the Dow Jones Industrial Average fluctuated between 1:1 and 2:1: Investors were willing to buy shares at prices up to twice the value of net assets recorded on balance sheets. Figure 10.1 illustrates how net assets encapsulated most of the perceived value of these firms.

The ratio rose dramatically over the next decade, reaching 6:1 at the height of the 1999 Internet and telecom frenzy. Remember, these stocks are not dot-com start-ups but 30 large, established U.S. companies. Sometime during the Reagan administration investors began to give credit to firms that invested in research and development (R&D), worker training, brand development, reengineering, and similar initiatives. Some of corporate America's countless advertising campaigns, patents, quality circles, and information technology initiatives delivered results. Even after the bubble burst the ratio remained at a historically high 3:1.

Certain firms grow profitably in the face of mature markets. A few great companies defy financial gravity and earn economic profit over decades. Rarely do physical assets distinguish these winners. They typically possess valuable brand, culture, knowledge, relationships, or other intangible assets that convey lower costs or greater pricing power. Compared to average companies, winning firms use these skills to drive larger wedges between price and cost.[2]

Wal-Mart's employee training, inventory systems, and supplier relationships allowed the retailer to earn consistent profits despite charging "Always Low Prices." Nordstrom's elite brand and attentive service allowed the retailer to charge higher prices. Some firms charge premium prices and incur lower costs. In the 1990s U.S. consumers paid higher prices for Toyota cars due to brand strength while the company simultaneously enjoyed lower manufacturing costs from superior shop floor practices.

Companies endowed with sustainable competitive advantage can be expected to generate cash flows that are greater, sooner, and more certain than those of less fortunate competitors. Information suggesting the presence of intangible assets could be extremely helpful to investors.

Consider Microsoft's condensed balance sheet as of June 30, 2002. Microsoft had a $50 billion book value and $300 billion market capitalization. Any firm trading at a 6:1 price-to-book ratio in 2002, the third consecutive year of an equity bear market, had to be doing something right. Yet the collection of assets recorded on the balance sheet included just cash, an equity portfolio, some receivables and buildings, and not much else. As shown in Table 10.1, total recorded intangible assets were valued at just $1.7 billion, less than 1 percent of the company's market value.

There was clearly something extraordinary about Microsoft, a firm whose software ran perhaps 90 percent of the world's personal computers and whose stock was the most valued on earth (highest market capitalization). However, reported assets gave little indication of its unique collection of skills and earnings power.

The accounting problem with intangible assets is not relevance but reliability. Every firm has skills. A McKinsey consultant, Goldman banker, and Wachtell attorney impress in varied ways. No accountant has developed a reliable means of valuing these organizations' internally developed knowledge without a market transaction. Of these three elite firms, only Goldman Sachs went public and provided such price discovery.

The Committee on Accounting Procedure (CAP) first addressed this issue with Bulletin 24, *Intangible Assets*, in December 1944. CAP distinguished (1) purchased intangibles from those developed internally and (2) those with finite lives (e.g., patents and licenses) from those with indefinite lives (e.g., goodwill and *perpetual* franchises). The Bulletin provided no guidance for valuing intangibles developed internally through "research, experimentation, advertising or otherwise."[3]

**Table 10.1   Condensed Balance Sheet for
Microsoft Corporation at June 30, 2002 ($ millions)**

Cash and marketable securities	$38,652	Accounts payable	$ 1,208
Accounts receivable	5,129	Unearned revenue	7,743
Other current assets	4,795	Income taxes payable	2,022
Property and equipment	2,268	Other liabilities	4,493
Equity investments	14,191	Total liabilities	15,466
Goodwill and intangible assets	1,669		
Other assets	942	Shareholders' equity	52,180
Total assets	$67,646	Liabilities and equity	$67,646

The Committee opined that intangibles acquired from third parties should be treated like any other asset: initial valuation at cost, systematic amortization over periods benefited, and write-down in case of impairment. Intangible assets with indefinite lives should be carried at historical cost until such time when the firm deems the asset to have a finite life, at which point it should be amortized or written down.

An interesting quirk of Bulletin 24 was that large write-offs of purchased intangibles could bypass the income statement and be charged to shareholders' equity to avoid misleading investors about the firm's earnings power. In other words, big-bath intangible write-offs could receive private balance sheet burials instead of public income statement funerals.

The next effort to reduce diversity of practice came with APB Opinion 17, also titled *Intangible Assets,* issued in August 1970. As with CAP, the APB framed the problem in terms of a two-by-two matrix, this time with intangible assets developed internally versus acquired from third parties and by identifiable intangibles such as patents, franchises, and trademarks versus unidentifiable goodwill.

Goodwill arises when a buying company acquires a firm for more than the fair market value of the target's identifiable tangible and intangible assets. Accountants allocate the remaining purchase price to goodwill, unobservable resources such as corporate culture, supplier relationships, brand equity, and anything else the buyer believes the target used to earn above-average profits. Academic researchers have found that purchased goodwill can be statistically significant in explaining share prices.

The big change, however, was that the APB concluded that all intangibles have finite lives and should be amortized over the estimated period benefited, not to exceed 40 years. Where does 40 years come from? The APB considered this selection a *practical* solution, reasoning that every intangible asset value must eventually drop to zero. Customers die, tastes change, suppliers go out of business, patents expire, laws evolve, and innovations emerge. The 40-year rule simply reduced diversity of practice. Amortization of goodwill influences reported periodic income, not cash flows.

Four of the 18 1970 APB members dissented with Opinion 17. Inflation accounting champion Sidney Davidson believed the arbitrary 40-year rule could never be appropriate in all circumstances. These dissenters preferred amortization periods based on professional judgment instead of bright-line rules. Auditors and regulators probably took comfort in the crisp 40-year time frame.

Opinion 17 gave no guidance on internally developed, identifiable intangible assets. In October 1974, the FASB issued Statement 2, *Accounting for Research and Development Costs.* With unanimous support of its seven members, the nascent FASB put forth the most concise standard in U.S. GAAP:

> All research and development costs encompassed by this Statement shall be charged to expense when incurred.[4]

The Statement also required companies to classify and disclose in its footnotes all R&D costs charged to expense in each accounting period.

The objective was to reduce diversity of accounting practices across corporate R&D efforts. A figure cited by the FASB suggested that more than 2 percent of U.S. gross domestic product (GDP) was spent by public and private sector organizations on R&D. The FASB chose to require immediate expensing because of uncertainty of future benefits arising from individual R&D projects and the lack of demonstrated causal relationship between R&D spending and future revenue.

Harvard Business School's Robert Anthony cited comments the FASB received as evidence of diversity of opinion on accounting practice. Three academics agreed with the Board, 11 did not; six accounting firms agreed, three did not; 34 businesses agreed, 17 did not. Imagine, Anthony suggested, problems to be encountered resolving more difficult, complex accounting issues.[5]

Eugene Flegm, as deputy assistant controller of General Motors, called Statement 2 the worst standard ever established because it eliminated management judgment and mandated a single standard in the absence of any clear abuse.[6]

Judgment still arose from determining the boundaries of R&D from more mundane activity. The FASB defined *research* as investigation aimed at discovery of new knowledge and *development* as translation of research findings into a new product or process. In bringing up a new machine, where along the continuum from prototype development to routine overhaul should accountants stop expensing and start capitalizing disbursements?

Pharmaceutical companies have enormous R&D programs. Successful drug companies trade at high price-to-book values because the market implicitly capitalizes previously expensed R&D disbursements when valuing shares. In other words, investors believe GAAP understates these firms' net assets.

Rising significance of software development motivated the SEC to issue a moratorium on changes in accounting policies associated with computer programming costs. Software can have value, and much of this intangible asset is developed internally. The

FASB issued Statement 86, *Accounting for the Costs of Computer Software to Be Sold, Leased, or Otherwise Marketed*, in August 1985.

Statement 86 required companies to expense R&D costs up until the point that *technological feasibility* had been established for a project. Thereafter, all software production costs should be capitalized on the balance sheet and amortized over the project's estimated economic life. Capitalized costs should be reported at the lower of amortized cost or net realizable value. Some have trouble reconciling why the FASB decided to expense all R&D but then established an exception for software development.

Ten years later, on July 5, 1995, IBM paid $3.2 billion in cash to acquire Lotus Development Corporation, a leading provider of business application software. In describing accounting policies, IBM's 1995 annual report said that management capitalized software costs incurred subsequent to establishment of technological feasibility. This policy clearly conformed to Statement 86.

An independent appraisal firm was retained by IBM to express an opinion on the fair market value of Lotus's assets and the purchase price allocation among resources acquired. The appraiser determined that fair market value of tangible assets acquired (e.g., cash, receivables, land, buildings, and equipment) represented 10 percent of the purchase price. The appraiser then determined two-thirds of the remaining purchase price represented *purchased in-process research and development* that had not reached the stage of technological feasibility. IBM expensed $1.8 billion of the $3.2 billion purchase price.

By July 1995, there was no doubt Lotus' software, including the blockbuster Notes electronic bulletin board and well-known 123 spreadsheet program, was in widespread use. Almost every person working at my employer in July 1995 used both tools daily. By any standard, Lotus had developed a suite of software products that had achieved technological feasibility. Yet IBM allocated just $290 million (9 percent) of the purchase price to current software products.

A cynical explanation is that management sought a tool to

smooth future earnings. By taking a huge one-time charge, management could depress the base of reported earnings and avoid having to amortize capitalized expenses in future accounting periods. Sometimes called spring-loading,[7] a one-time charge helps a firm show subsequent earnings growth after the new sheriff enters town.

In June 2001 the FASB released Statement 142, *Goodwill and Other Intangible Assets.* Once again, standard setters did not address accounting for internally developed intangible assets. Instead, the Statement focused on allocation of purchase price to tangible and intangible assets obtained through purchase, merger, or acquisition.

Whereas Opinion 17 concluded that all intangibles are wasting assets with finite lives, Statement 142 concluded that goodwill and other intangible assets have indefinite lives and should not be amortized arbitrarily. Intangibles should be tested for impairment at least annually, and any identified impairment should be charged to income. Statement 142 relieved companies from intangible amortization's drag on future earnings but created the prospect of volatile earnings from unanticipated impairment.

To this day, accounting standard setters have not determined how to value internally developed intangible assets other than software. This issue's most interesting case study is that of Internet service provider America Online. AOL's big innovation in the mid-1990s was mailing unsolicited, free disks to households with personal computers.

AOL gave Main Street America early Internet access through telephone lines. The scrappy upstart spent heavily to enroll millions of subscribers and grow quickly. Publicly traded firms needing more financing feel enormous pressure to report consistent profits. Bill Sharpe's arguments about diversifiable risk mean little to aspiring corporate treasurers.

AOL's solution? Capitalize acquisition costs on the balance

sheet and amortize them over periods of up to 24 months. At June 30, 1995, AOL had total assets of $405 million, of which $77 million (19 percent) were *deferred subscriber acquisition costs*. A year later, this balance ballooned to $314, or one-third of the company's balance sheet. If AOL had expensed these costs, it would have reported losses.

Accountants shy away from capitalizing intangible asset development costs. No one knows how to match these costs with uncertain future revenues. The financial accounting policy of AOL became the subject of business school case studies and an SEC investigation. The SEC charged that AOL failed to demonstrate ability to recover acquisition costs through future revenues. In May 2000 AOL agreed to a $3.5 million fine and to restate 1995 and 1996 earnings.

AOL then grew through a series of remarkably bold acquisitions. Its soaring stock price created a currency to buy significant companies. The capstone event came in January 2001 when AOL used its overvalued stock to acquire media giant Time Warner in the largest corporate acquisition to date, a transaction described by one critic as a company without assets buying another without a clue.[8]

AOL Time Warner's resulting 2001 balance sheet represented Goodwill Central: of $208 billion of assets, $128 billion (62 percent) represented goodwill. The balance sheet also showed $11 billion of brand and trademark assets plus $27 billion in cable television and sports franchise assets.

The FASB issued Statement 142 and required testing goodwill for impairment in fiscal years beginning after January 1, 2002. For the quarter ending March 31, 2002, management wrote off $54 billion of goodwill, an amount one journalist cited as the GDP of Ecuador. Even after the write-down, the firm still had $80 billion of goodwill and $45 billion of other intangible assets.

A write-off suggests prior period results showed too much profit because assets' useful lives turned out not to be as long as previously estimated. In 1975 fewer than 5 percent of public companies reported a large write-off; in 1994, 21 percent did so.[9]

According to Goldman Sachs' Abby Joseph Cohen, in 2002 corporate America paid the price for its 1990s acquisitions binge and recognized $140 billion of intangible write-offs, a sum equal to write-offs of the previous eight years.[10]

Aside from LIFO, the biggest quirk in American financial reporting was pooling-of-interests accounting for business combinations. The term emerged in the 1943 *Niagara Falls Power Company v. Federal Power Commission* (137 F.2d 787) decision written by Learned Hand. A water utility had been formed from the 1918 combination of two predecessor firms that contributed stock to create a new, successor organization. The predecessor firms did not sell their stock and the successor firm did not purchase shares from either party. Each of the predecessor firms retained an interest in the new company.

A dispute arose over the value of the combined plant. Lower asset values, based on historical costs, would limit the successor firm's ability to secure rate increases. The Federal Power Commission, seeking low water prices, argued that no sale had taken place and historical cost was the appropriate asset valuation. The utility company believed that the business combination represented a transaction that allowed assets to be marked to fair value at the time of the combination.

Justice Hand opined that the two old companies had pooled their interests. From that time forward the firms needed to treat as vested the asset values they then happened to have. There was no basis for recognizing an arm's-length transaction that would give rise to asset revaluation. If there had been a customary transaction, purchase accounting would have adjusted assets to fair value and combined income statements from the acquisition date.

Pooling differs from purchase accounting in three ways. Poolings (1) add balance sheets and income statements from the beginning of the year, (2) generate higher reported revenues and earnings (a pooling transaction consummated on

December 31 would still show 12 months of combined revenues and income), and (3) spare the new entity's income statement depreciation charges from stepped-up asset values. The choice between pooling and purchase treatment has no influence on cash flows.

Experience with the pooling versus purchase debate shows that neither principles nor rules are magic bullets required to solve standard setting disputes. The Committee on Accounting Procedure issued Bulletin 40, *Business Combinations*, in September 1950. The ARB suggested that pooling treatment should be used when predecessor firms were of comparable size, in similar lines of business, and showed continuity of ownership and management. The Committee reiterated these guidelines in Bulletin 48 seven years later, as did the APB with Opinion 10 in 1966.

Niagara Power's bad news turned into a windfall for conglomerate managers and their investment bankers. Wall Street helped CEOs use pooling treatment to combine organizations of disparate size and lines of business to report brilliant earnings trajectories. Conglomerates and their auditors ignored accounting guidelines. Some acquisitions using pooling represented less than 1 percent of the size of the buying firm. Management simply wanted to facilitate instant creation of earnings.[11]

The University of Illinois' Art Wyatt wrote a 1963 research paper critical of pooling accounting. Four years later, Baruch College's Abraham Briloff, perhaps the industry's most famous gadfly, wrote a widely read article titled "Dirty Pooling."[12] Briloff demonstrated how pooling treatment could mislead investors. The paper's most famous line was that accounting statements are like bikinis: what they show is interesting but what they conceal is significant.

To curtail abuse, the APB substituted rules for principles with Opinion 16 in 1970. The APB imposed 12 conditions to be satisfied before pooling accounting could be used. Creative bankers responded by constructing transactions to satisfy the constraints. An unintended consequence was that target firms gained bargaining power if suitors sought pooling treatment.

Obsession with reported earnings led some management teams to go to extraordinary lengths to use pooling accounting. AT&T's $7.5 billion acquisition of NCR Corporation in September 1991 required management to overcome five obstacles to comply with the requirements of Opinion 16. AT&T incurred substantial economic cost to avoid recognizing about $5 billion of goodwill or $125 million of annual noncash amortization for the next 40 years.[13]

On April 21, 1999, the FASB announced it would eliminate pooling-of-interests accounting for business combinations. Stock returns of companies known to use pooling showed a 3 percent abnormal stock market decline immediately after the announcement. On December 20, 2000, the FASB announced that goodwill arising from purchase accounting need no longer be amortized. Stock returns for a sample of firms with substantial amounts of goodwill enjoyed an abnormal 2 percent increase.[14]

These results, at odds with the idea that investors care more about cash than reported earnings, illustrate the messiness of financial markets: no one can make sweeping generalizations about the efficient markets hypothesis with confidence. However, other research provides evidence that shareholders of buying firms did not consider financial reporting effects of pooling to be beneficial.[15]

11

DEBT

Practitioners showed little interest in the efficient markets hypothesis. A consequence is that many statement preparers believed outside creditors and investors could be fooled by the "optics" of financial statement presentation. Balance sheet form could seemingly trump economic substance when analysts evaluated a company's health. This belief manifested itself most clearly in accounting for debt on the balance sheet. The presence of debt came to be viewed as a sign of corporate weakness. Management teams pushed standard setters to permit companies to keep debt off of balance sheet presentation.

A balance sheet's left-hand side displays assets recognized by accounting convention. The right-hand side apportions asset ownership among creditors and owners. Creditors may wrest control from owners if a firm fails to make timely payment for obligations owed. The fraction of a firm's asset base financed through liabilities is perhaps the most significant issue in corporate finance.

Creditor obligations have finite lives, whereas shareholders' residual claims extend over a corporation's indefinite life. Owners may receive interim dividend payments, but the firm has no contractual obligation to make these distributions. Shareholders get their money back when they sell shares to other investors in a secondary market or when the firm retires the equity through share repurchase or liquidation. Equity holders bear more risk than creditors and demand higher financial returns.

The U.S. tax code since 1894 has permitted interest expense deductions when computing a corporation's taxable income. The tax code makes no such provision for dividend distributions to investors. The deductibility of interest makes a firm's capital structure, the share of long-term financing allocated between debt and equity, a determinant of firm value. Some debt gives the firm protection against income taxes; too much exposes the firm to bankruptcy.

Imagine a firm requiring $5 million of long-term financing that generates $2 million in operating income annually. Suppose owners can finance the enterprise with varied levels of debt at a constant interest rate. Notice in Table 11.1 that the absolute level of net income drops with the addition of debt financing but that the share of earnings retained by both debt and equity investors increases (amounts in thousands, except per share figures).

Debt financing provides a tax shield and allows capital providers to retain a greater share of the firm's earnings. Substituting debt for equity reduces the number of outstanding shares of common stock and thus raises earnings per share (EPS). Some believe debt further enhances firm value because discipline required to repay borrowings deters ill-conceived investments.

**Table 11.1 Debt Creates a Tax Shield and
Concentrates Earnings among Fewer Shares**

	Amount of Debt in Capital Structure		
	None	Some	Lots
Debt	$ 0	$1,500	$4,000
Shareholders' equity, $1 par value	5,000	3,500	1,000
Total capital	$5,000	$5,000	$5,000
Operating earnings	$2,000	$2,000	$2,000
Interest expense at 8%	0	(120)	(320)
Earnings before taxes	2,000	1,880	1,680
Income taxes at 35%	(700)	(658)	(588)
Net income	$1,300	$1,222	$1,092
Operating earnings	$2,000	$2,000	$2,000
Tax payment to government	(700)	(658)	(588)
Earnings retained by debt and equity investors	1,300	1,342	1,412
Annual income tax shield provided by debt	$ 0	$ 42	$ 112
Earnings per share of common stock	$ 0.26	$ 0.35	$ 1.09

Beyond some point, however, additional debt causes problems. The threat of large, recurring interest payments may prevent firm owners from spending money on advertising, maintenance, employee training, or research and development.

The prospect of financial distress causes lenders to worry that owners could act counter to creditors' interests. Shareholders of overly levered firms may salvage positions at the expense of bondholders. Tactics include declaring large cash dividends and leaving fewer assets to lenders in the event of a liquidation; issuing even more debt, which makes old debt riskier and less valuable; selling valuable assets, which leaves creditors less collateral to back their loans; or swinging for the fences with a risky investment, when bondholders would have been better off if management simply liquidated the firm.

$$\succ$$

In the 1960s, Michael Milken, a Phi Beta Kappa graduate of Berkeley and star Wharton MBA student, formed a breathtakingly simple conclusion. The bond market was fully capable of pricing credit risk of highly leveraged corporations. Bond investors holding a diversified portfolio of so-called junk debt could mitigate company-specific exposures and earn an appropriate return. On the other side, nonprime borrowers could bypass banks and insurance companies and sell debt directly to bondholders at lower cost. Debt issuance had been the preserve of established corporations with investment-grade credit ratings.

Milken joined a moribund Philadelphia investment bank in 1969 and worked tirelessly to create a loyal following of high-yield debt investors. He then helped issuers securitize high-yield borrowings, parsing risky loans into divisible $1,000 bonds that could be traded in secondary markets. Finally, he worked with his revitalized employer, Drexel Burnham Lambert, to make a market in these bonds so queasy bondholders could sell positions easily. Milken's career soared.

Milken showed an uncanny ability to design capital structures to support diverse businesses with heavy debt loads. Securities partition cash distributions and voting rights among capital providers. Capital structure establishes the sequence and conditions required for each set of investors and creditors to receive such rights.

Using building blocks of debt, equity, and options, Milken crafted sophisticated hybrid securities that satisfied needs of varied stakeholders. He also received warrants from many debt issuers; these long-term options allowed Milken to capture some of the upside potential as heavy borrowers paid off massive debt loads.

He also benefited from circumstance. The 1981 tax law allowed companies to depreciate fixed assets even faster than permitted by the 1954 tax code revision. The larger tax shield let corporations devote more cash flow to debt service and borrow greater sums. Recent savings and loan deregulation permitted thrifts to invest in junk bonds. Relaxed enforcement of antitrust laws by the Reagan administration allowed companies to use debt to acquire firms in the same industry.[1]

Some believed blossoming use of debt could solve the agency problem of managers acting at odds with owners' interests. The argument was that large cash flows thrown off by mature corporations were an invitation to mischief when management had little ownership interest in the company. Instead of returning cash to investors and creditors, inattentive managers would lavish money on perquisites and disastrous diversification projects.

Substantial use of debt financing could discipline errant management. Large interest obligations would force managers to pare expenses and improve operating efficiency. Leveraged buyout (LBO) artists borrowed lots of money using the target company's assets and cash flow as security, paid a premium for old shareholders' stock, and took companies private. These financiers motivated management teams to work harder by sharing ownership of the now-private company. Judicious use of debt, the argument went, could transform flabby American corporations into leaner, more competitive firms on the world stage.

Early successes gave way to hostile takeovers—unfriendly LBOs—in the 1980s. Using junk-bond financing, T. Boone Pickens tried to take over Gulf Oil; Saul Steinberg sought control of Disney; Carl Icahn, Phillips Petroleum; Sir James Goldsmith, Crown Zellerbach; and so on. Drexel learned how to raise billions of dollars in days from its bond investor network. The pinnacle came with Kohlberg Kravis Roberts & Co.'s $26 billion buyout of RJR Nabisco.

Extreme use of debt fell into disfavor in the 1990s. An ambitious U.S. Attorney named Rudolph Giuliani helped bring down the Milken empire with charges of insider trading and other security law violations. Some LBOs failed because cash flows could not support crushing debt burdens. And critics gained traction arguing that takeovers by management teams without industry expertise tended to impair efficiency and starve firms of needed research and development, equipment modernization, and advertising.[2]

In the 1990s, debt, or at least the appearance of substantial debt financing, came to be viewed as a sign of weakness. Great companies had pricing power, lean cost structures, effective advertising, and global distribution channels. Robust earnings obviated the need for debt financing.

One barometer of public opinion was the annual *Fortune* magazine's list of most admired corporations. Table 11.2 lists firms appearing more than once in the top 10 list during the 1990s together with the concurrent Standard & Poor's rating on each firm's unsecured debt. Not one of these firms had junk debt ratings, and the most admired firms—Coca-Cola, Procter & Gamble, and Merck—maintained fortress balance sheets.

Investors and journalists likely viewed debt as a sign of weakness: healthy companies didn't need tax shields to create value. Some management teams tried to reduce the amount of debt reported on company balance sheets and increase apparent borrowing capacity. Leases, litigation, contingencies, and consolidations attracted standard setters' attention.

A common form of debt is leasing. A fixed asset owner, known as a lessor, rents real estate, equipment, or other property in exchange for payments made by a lessee. Rental payments compensate asset owners for wear and tear plus financing costs. Leases can extend from a couple of hours for a set of golf clubs to a century for a plot of land.

The accounting issue is determining when a leasing transaction morphs from a rental to a financed sale. No one believes renting a car for one day constitutes ownership; however, the issue becomes less clear if the contract continues for weeks, months, or years. Past some point, the lessee controls the property

Table 11.2 Debt Ratings of Companies Appearing More Than Once in *Fortune's* List of 10 Most Admired Companies

Company	1990	1991	1992	1993	1994	1995	1996	1997	1998	1999
Coca-Cola	AA	AA	AA	AA	AA	AA	AA	AA-	AA-	A+
Procter & Gamble	AA+	AA	AA	AA	AA	AA	AA	AA		
Merck	AAA	AAA	AAA	AAA			AAA	AAA	AAA	AAA
Rubbermaid	BBB+	BBB+	A-	A	A	A	A			
Microsoft					[No debt]	[No debt]	AA	AA	AA	AA
3M	AAA	AAA	AAA	AAA	AAA	AAA				
Wal-Mart	AA	AA	AA	AA						AA
Johnson & Johnson		AAA	AAA				AAA	AAA	AAA	
Intel						A+	A+	A+	A+	A+
PepsiCo	A	A	A							
Liz Claiborne		[No debt]	[No debt]	[No debt]						
United Parcel Service					AAA	AAA		AAA		
Motorola					AA	AA	AA			
Disney					[Not rated]	AA	AA			A
Hewlett-Packard									A	A
Berkshire Hathaway						AA+	AA+		AA+	
Boeing		AA		AA			AAA	AAA	AAA	AAA
Levi Strauss			[Not rated]	[Not rated]						
JP Morgan				A	A					
Home Depot					A	A+				
Mirage Resorts							BBB+	BBB+		
General Electric									AAA	AAA
Southwest Airlines									A-	A-

Source of data: Fortune magazine, 1990–1999.

and should show the asset and corresponding financing liability on its balance sheet.

Companies concerned with appearance of debt on balance sheets do not want to do this. Accounting standard setters, in contrast, want lessees to be very clear about disclosing debt obligations. The accounting decision to capitalize the lease on the balance sheet or just report lease expenses through the income statement has no effect on cash flow. Over the life of the asset, accounting treatment makes no difference.

To illustrate the point, suppose a firm leased a $15,000 machine at the beginning of 1976. The equipment owner charged annual rental payments to recover its 6 percent borrowing rate plus straight-line depreciation over the asset's five-year useful life. If the user accounted for the transaction as a capital lease, then it would show both a $15,000 asset and a $15,000 loan. Both balances would be amortized over the five-year life: the asset through depreciation and the loan through repayment. If the user accounted for the contract as an operating lease, then the firm would simply record a lease expense each year. Table 11.3 shows both operating lease and capital lease accounting treatment.

Under either accounting treatment the firm pays $3,561 annually for five years. Cash flows remain unaffected. Accounting for the transaction as a capital lease raises the amount of debt shown on the balance sheet and front-loads interest expense in earlier years. Financial statements under lease capitalization do not look as attractive in the early years of a contract. However, by the end of 1980, cumulative cash payments and incurred expenses add to $17,805. Choice of accounting policy simply affects reported income and debt levels on interim financial statements.

Accounting Series Release 147 issued by the SEC in 1973 required lessees to disclose the present value of lease payments for long-term leases not capitalized. The newly formed FASB took up accounting for leases as an early priority. During its first seven years, the FASB devoted half of its staff resources to lease accounting issues.[3]

**Table 11.3   Equivalence of Operating
and Capital Leases over Life of Asset**

	Loan Amortization Schedule					
	Beginning Balance	Interest Expense	Annual Payment	Reduction in Loan	Ending Balance	Annual Depreciation
1976	$15,000	$ 900	$ (3,561)	$ (2,661)	$12,339	$ 3,000
1977	12,339	740	(3,561)	(2,821)	9,518	3,000
1978	9,518	571	(3,561)	(2,990)	6,529	3,000
1979	6,529	392	(3,561)	(3,169)	3,359	3,000
1980	3,359	202	(3,561)	(3,359)	0	3,000
		$2,805	$(17,805)	$(15,000)		$15,000

	Capital Lease			Operating	
	Interest +	Depreciation =	Total	Lease	Difference
1976	$ 900	$ 3,000	$ 3,900 −	$ 3,561 =	$339
1977	740	3,000	3,740	3,561	179
1978	571	3,000	3,571	3,561	10
1979	392	3,000	3,392	3,561	(169)
1980	202	3,000	3,202	3,561	(359)
	$2,805	$15,000	$17,805	$17,805	$ 0

Statement 13, *Accounting for Leases,* issued in November 1976, represents the ultimate rules-based accounting standard. For lessees, a contract satisfying any of four criteria is deemed a capital lease; if not, it is an operating lease where the asset and loan obligation are kept off the balance sheet. The most important of the four tests was whether the present value of lease payments summed to more than 90 percent of the asset's fair market value. Any enterprising deal maker could make the numbers work to avoid lease capitalization.

The FASB commissioned a postimplementation review of Statement 13. A research team of nine academics studied companies that used and did not use leases before and after implementation of Statement 13. They analyzed financial statements, surveyed finance professionals, performed in-depth interviews, and studied stock and bond returns.

The team found Statement 13 caused companies to structure contracts to avoid capitalization. Firms renegotiated existing leases to ensure assets and debt stayed off balance sheets. Yet financial markets seemed unimpressed by such window dressing: the research team found that capitalizing leases under Statement 13 had no identifiable, adverse effect on bond yields or stock prices. Managers simply worried that capitalizing leases would influence perceptions of financial statement users.[4]

Twenty years later such sentiment endured. Union Pacific opened a new headquarters building in 2004 under an operating lease that guaranteed 89.9 percent of construction costs. On the Sun Microsystems web site, a finance division promoted leasing "as a way to keep the asset off your balance sheet" to "circumvent the restrictive covenants imposed by many banks." An auto leasing company web page said that operating leases make "your financial statements look better to a banker."[5]

An interesting contrast to lease accounting was the March 1975 issuance of Statement 5, *Accounting for Contingencies.* Uncertain circumstances whose subsequent resolution can give rise to a loss represent contingencies. Pending litigation and guaranteeing others' debts are notable examples. The accounting problem is determining when, if ever, to recognize contingent outcomes in financial statements.

The FASB concluded that companies should accrue for contingent losses if the outcome is both probable and estimable. No bright-line tests exist for either standard. Accountants must use individual judgment when recognizing and valuing contingent losses.

Not surprisingly, firms showed inconsistent accounting treatment. A 1997 study of environmental cleanup exposures showed more prevalent disclosure among larger firms and those reporting lower profits.[6] A 2004 survey of 600 firms showed that just 295 presented a caption for contingencies in the balance sheet even though all of them likely faced meaningful litigation exposure.[7]

The point is that within a year the FASB issued a standard based on strict rules and another based on general principles. As with the debate on pooling of interests, critics found problems with both rules and principles, suggesting that neither preparer judgment nor explicit regulation is the answer to financial accounting policy issues.

Further evidence that firms strive to keep reported debt off balance sheets is the glacial pace of establishing a standard for consolidations. Consolidated statements present financial positions and operating results for a parent and its subsidiaries or affiliates as if the group were a single economic entity.

The reasoning is that a consolidated perspective, combining disparate assets, liabilities, revenues, and expenses into one whole, gives shareholders and creditors a more meaningful perspective than if the units had been reported separately. Critics of consolidation argue that combining apples and oranges from different balance sheets obscures financial positions.

Until 1993 retailer Sears owned Allstate Insurance. Sears held a massive inventory of household goods, whereas Allstate held a huge investment portfolio; Sears' liabilities included debt, whereas Allstate's included industry-specific line items such as unearned premiums and unpaid claims. Reasonable minds could differ about the appropriateness of consolidating these two operations in Sears' financial statements. Arthur Lowes Dickinson demanded that U.S. Steel present consolidated figures before Price Waterhouse certified the financial statements in 1903.

Management teams shy away from presenting consolidated figures because combination almost always adds debt to the balance sheet. More debt suggests reduced borrowing capacity and diminished financial strength.

One way to assess the amount of debt, also known as financial leverage, is to express outstanding debt as a fraction of long-term financing such as debt and shareholders' equity.

Consider a manufacturer that created a financing subsidiary to lend customers money in support of equipment sales. The balance sheet of the manufacturing arm has inventory, property, plant, and equipment financed by payables and debt. The financing arm has loan receivables financed by debt. Table 11.4 shows how the manufacturer's investment in the financing subsidiary's net assets—called the equity method, otherwise known as a one-line consolidation—presents a slimmed-down balance sheet with financial leverage of 29 percent.

If the manufacturer consolidates the financing arm into the balance sheet, and substitutes $280,000 of assets and $200,000 of liabilities for the $80,000 investment in net assets, then the balance sheet balloons. Nothing economically has changed about the combined entity, but reported financial leverage grows to 55 percent. The subsidiary's equity cannot be

**Table 11.4   Two Ways to Report a
Manufacturing Operation with a Financing Subsidiary**

		Combined Firm	
	Financing Subsidiary	*Equity Method*	*Full Consolidation*
Cash	$ 15,000	$ 15,000	$ 30,000
Receivables	—	50,000	50,000
Inventory	—	75,000	75,000
Consumer loans	250,000	—	250,000
Investment in financing subsidiary	—	80,000	—
Plant and equipment	15,000	180,000	195,000
Total assets	$280,000	$400,000	$600,000
Accounts payable	—	$ 50,000	$ 50,000
Debt	200,000	**100,000**	**$300,000**
Total liabilities	200,000	150,000	350,000
Shareholders' equity	80,000	250,000	250,000
Liabilities and shareholders' equity	$280,000	$400,000	$600,000
Financial Leverage: Debt/(Debt & Equity) =		**29%**	**55%**

carried forward to the consolidated balance sheet because financing for ownership came from the parent's shareholders and creditors.

The accounting issue is deciding when circumstances warrant consolidation of assets and liabilities. U.S. financial accounting standard setters touched this topic once. In August 1959 the Committee on Accounting Procedure issued Bulletin 51, *Consolidated Financial Statements.* In one of the few bright-line rules promulgated by CAP, a corporation should generally consolidate assets and liabilities of subsidiaries when it owns more than 50 percent of the voting shares of the subsidiary. The IRS uses an 80 percent threshold before requiring consolidation of subsidiary tax returns.

Consolidated balance sheets are not as pretty. Many CFOs would rather push off debt to unconsolidated related parties. A famous example was Coca-Cola's 1986 "49 percent solution," when CFO M. Douglas Ivester orchestrated the 51 percent spin-off of U.S. bottling operations into Coca-Cola Enterprises (CCE).

Coke removed $2.4 billion of debt from its balance sheet yet continued to exert de facto control over bottling operations through command of six subsidiary board seats. Under Coke's direction, CCE borrowed more money to finance purchases of independent bottlers. The new debt stayed off Coke's balance sheet. This structure also allowed Coke to record additional revenue by raising prices of soda concentrate sold to CCE.[8]

Despite criticism that the 50 percent rule was a blunt instrument, the Accounting Principles Board did not address consolidations during its 20-year history. The FASB embarked on a consolidations project in January 1982 and has yet to issue a definitive statement after more than two decades.

In October 1987 the FASB issued Statement 94, which tightened enforcement of Bulletin 51 and required consolidation of majority-owned subsidiaries that were *nonhomogeneous,* such as insurance, real estate, and leasing subsidiaries. The FASB used Statement 94 as an interim measure to reduce the incidence of off-balance-sheet financing.

➢

Debt confers some benefit to corporations. Experiences of the 1980s, however, showed debt to be a treacherous servant. Management teams preparing financial statements became loath to report debt on balance sheets. Both rules and principles put forth by standard setters proved only modestly effective in forcing statement preparers to acknowledge the scope of corporate obligations. This shortcoming would come back to haunt investors and creditors during the telecom bubble.

12

OPTIONS

Incentives are the cornerstone of modern life. And understanding them—or, often, ferreting them out—is the key to solving just about any riddle.

—Steven D. Levitt and Stephen J. Dubner, *Freakonomics*

The third great idea in the history of finance was development of the Black-Scholes option pricing model. The previous chapter showed how debt rose into and then fell out of favor with corporate management and their boards. This chapter describes how compensation with options replaced debt as a governance tool in the 1990s.

Valuation complexity made accounting for option contracts a tricky matter. The Black-Scholes model allowed accountants to resolve a long-standing debate, yet practitioners remained slow to embrace this tool. Corporations did not charge options-based compensation expenses to income statements.

Financial accounting thus enabled some corporate boards to make outlandish use of this compensation tool. Options represent leveraged assets, where modest changes in stock prices can have substantial influence on option values. Further, unlike the indefinite life of stock, option contracts expire. Option recipients' preoccupation with short-term movements in their employer's stock prices contributed to the accounting meltdown in 2002.

Imagine you owned a gold mine when extraction and mining costs equaled gold's market price of $400 per ounce. Mining gold would yield zero accounting profit. A neighbor offers to take the mine off your hands for a dollar. Would you accept the offer? Probably not. The price of gold could subsequently rise so mining would become profitable. This possibility is likely worth more than a dollar.

Owning a mine represents an option. The mine owner has the opportunity without the obligation to spend money to extract gold. If gold's price holds steady or drops, then the option remains unexercised. If the price rises, the owner may choose to exercise the option and realize a profit.

Option holders have the right to buy or sell something in the future at a fixed price. If market value exceeds the contract's strike price, then a call option holder can realize a profit by either exercising the option or selling the unused contract to someone else. If the contract price exceeds the market price at the end of the contract term, nothing happens and the option expires worthless.

Companies sometimes use options as risk management tools. A growing firm unsure of future space needs could buy a call option for an attractive parcel of land. In exchange for a modest option premium, the firm ensures that the landowner will not sell the parcel to anyone else for a specified period of time. If growth materializes and the company needs more land, the firm exercises the option and buys the land at the previously agreed-upon strike price. If growth decelerates and there is no need for more space, the company lets the option expire.

Corporate boards often grant options to executives in an effort to align management interests with those of owners. A rising stock price increases stock option values and rewards both managers and owners. In the 1980s boards used debt as a stick to align management interests with those of owners. In the 1990s, when debt fell into disfavor, directors used options as a carrot to motivate desired behavior.

Going back to the gold mine example, suppose the company's stock trades at $20 per share and an option holder can buy a share of stock for $20 up to one year from the date of the option grant. Figure 12.1 summarizes these facts.

When the market price equals the strike price, exercising the option yields a payoff of zero to the option holder. However, the holder could probably sell the contract for about $4. The difference between the exercise value and market value represents the time value of the unexercised option. The accounting problem has been measuring this difference.

Academics spent decades trying to solve this problem. Two Columbia professors writing in 1933 said that option contracts had not been traded long enough to permit formation of any

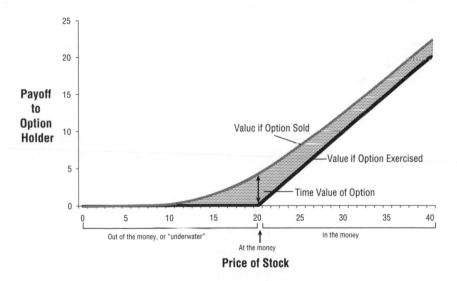

**Figure 12.1   Market Value versus Exercise Value
of a One-Year Call Option with a $20 Strike Price**

intelligent judgment of their value. Option valuation seemed inexplicable.[1]

A legal scholar writing in 1953 commented that executive compensation had declined in real purchasing power over the period from 1939 to 1951 due to wartime tax rates and inflation. Wage earners had done comparatively well during this period. Stock options then offered a tax-efficient means of restoring executive pay.

Unfortunately, after speaking with security analysts, investment bankers, option traders, and actuaries, the author remained unable to find anyone offering a viable means of valuing option grants. He concluded that there appeared to be no realistic method of arriving at a dollar value for a stock option.[2]

An accounting theorist writing in 1970 acknowledged there was no definitive way to value options. He offered several possibilities: compare the difference between market and exercise prices at various dates, look for market values of traded options, or estimate the value of the consideration given in exchange for the option grant.[3] Economic heavyweights like Paul Samuelson and Robert Merton could not find a general solution.

Standard-setting bodies had wrestled with option valuation since the 1940s, especially within the context of compensation. The Committee on Accounting Procedure (CAP) issued Bulletin 37, *Accounting for Compensation in the Form of Stock Options*, in November 1948, and published a revision in January 1953 after a tax law change minimized the amount of income taxable to employees from certain option awards. The CAP recognized that employee stock options constituted a form of compensation and that omission of resulting compensation expense may overstate employers' net income.

The Committee acknowledged that options have value beyond the difference between market and exercise price but claimed this balance was impractical to measure, especially when employees could not sell unexercised options. As a consequence the CAP did not require companies to recognize compensation expense if the option strike price equaled fair market value at the time of the grant.

In September 1960 Arthur Andersen & Co. wrote in a position paper that its management thought the difference between the share price and option strike price on the grant date understated a corporation's option compensation expense. The firm conceded that the absence of a precise valuation tool complicated financial reporting. The partners felt that a better, more practical approach was to charge to income an estimate for the difference between strike price and expected share price on the earliest date employees could exercise the options granted.[4]

In March 1969 the Accounting Principles Board (APB) considered whether convertible debt (corporate bonds issued with an option entitling bondholders to convert bonds into stock at a fixed price) should be accounted for simply as debt or a combination of a bond with a call option on stock with separate accounting treatment for each feature.

Unlike employee stock options granted at-the-money, convertible bonds have option strike prices set above the stock's fair market value at the time of issue. In exchange for giving bond investors a call option on company shares, the corporation receives a lower interest rate for its debt.

In Opinion 14, *Accounting for Convertible Debt and Debt Issued with Stock Purchase Warrants*, the APB concluded that valuation of the call option presented practical problems. In the absence of market prices for similar options, conversion terms could be valued only subjectively. The prudent action in the absence of reliable valuation was to attribute no portion of the convertible bond issue's proceeds to the call option.

The APB revisited option accounting again in October 1972, just months before publication of the seminal Black-Scholes article. Opinion 25, *Accounting for Stock Issued to Employees*, made technical adjustments to CAP's Bulletin 37 but continued to require stock option valuation to be the difference between market and strike price at the time of the grant.

In other words, at-the-money option grants bore no accounting charge for the option's time value. Of the 18 members of the 1972 APB, six assented with qualification and three dissented. In particular, Haskins & Sells partner Oscar Gellein, who had supervised the massive General Motors audit, opined that valuation problems could be resolved.[5]

Pieces fell into place in the spring of 1973. On April 26 the Chicago Board Options Exchange opened for business. Then the May–June issue of the *Journal of Political Economy* published "The Pricing of Options and Corporate Liabilities" by economists Fischer Black and Myron Scholes, who resorted to stochastic calculus and physics' heat transfer equation to solve the problem.[6] The business community received a workable option valuation tool plus a venue for trading standardized contracts.

Traders had long understood that option contracts represent leveraged investments. Small moves in underlying stock prices could have disproportionate influence on option values. Black and Scholes' insight was to decompose options into building blocks that could be more easily priced. Consider the following simplified replication strategy which breaks the option into two pieces: buying some stock and borrowing money at 10 percent to leverage the security's return.

Assume the gold mine's stock has a $20 price today, does not pay a dividend, and has an expected 40 percent annual standard deviation of returns (i.e., its volatility leads to a two-thirds chance that its share price will settle one year from now between $12 [$20 – (40% × $20)] and $28 [$20 + (40% × $20)].

Exercising the option in one year gives a payoff of $8 if the stock rises ($28 future market price – $20 exercise price) or $0 if it falls because underwater options expire worthless. Figure 12.2 presents these two outcomes.

Figure 12.2   Two Payoffs from a Call Option

These payoff functions permit decomposition into a share purchase and a borrowing:

Let *d* equal the number of shares to be purchased for replication.

Let *PV* equal the present value of borrowing required for replication.

Algebra presented in Table 12.1 solves two unknowns in two equations.

Implied option value = (Today's stock price)
(Number of shares required for replication) – (Present value of borrowing)
$$= (\$20)(0.5) - (\$5.45) = \$4.55 \text{ per option}$$

Table 12.1   Solving for Two Unknowns in Two Equations

Stock Move	Payoff Values	Transformation	Unknowns Solved
Rises	$28d - 1.10PV = \$8$➤	$28d - 1.10PV = 8$	
Falls	$12d - 1.10PV = \$0$➤	$-12d + 1.10PV = 0$	
		$16d \qquad\qquad = 8$	$[d = 0.5,\ PV = 5.45]$

Formal pricing models value this option closer to $4. Real-world constraints complicate employee option valuation: employees cannot sell options to third parties, they forfeit awards for leaving the company before vesting, and they must abstain from share trades during blackout periods before earnings releases. Such restrictions reduce employee option values relative to output from a model.

Nevertheless, Black and Scholes' work allowed accountants to value option contracts more easily than, say, pension obligations or deferred tax liabilities. The model represents the third great idea in finance. Accountants no longer had an excuse for failing to ascribe a value to option contracts.

Use of options in executive compensation gained momentum after a 1993 revision to the Internal Revenue Code. Section 162(m) disallowed deduction for annual salaries greater than $1 million paid to publicly traded firms' CEOs and its four other most highly compensated executive officers. Beginning in 1994 any compensation over the million-dollar limit had to be performance-based to qualify for a tax deduction. Stock options became the tool of choice to satisfy this condition.

Options appealed to cash-poor technology firms seeking to attract, motivate, and retain high-priced talent. Validation of this business model came from Silicon Valley's Class of 1986. Oracle, Sun Microsystems, Silicon Graphics, Adobe Systems, Informix, and Microsoft went public that year.[7] Thousands of employees became millionaires as employer stock prices rose.

Hope for similar riches allowed other start-ups to attract talented people. By one estimate corporations had set aside about $60 billion of stock for option awards in 1985; 12 years later the figure blossomed to $600 billion.[8] In 1970 CEO pay averaged 39 times an average worker's salary. By 1999, use of options had grown this multiple to a thousand.[9]

In the gold mine example, suppose the company's directors granted 100,000 options with a $20 strike price to a high-potential recruit. If, for example, the share price appreciated to $30, the lucky executive could exercise her options, sell stock in the open market, and pocket a million-dollar pretax return. Under Opinion 25 the mine would not have to recognize any compensation expense.

Opinion 25's treatment appears to give everybody a win. Managers get rich, shareholders enjoy fruits of motivated employees, CFOs avoid charges to earnings per share, and tax managers look productive because corporations could deduct share price appreciation on federal returns. However, few accountants believed this reporting mirrored economic reality.

A preferred accounting treatment would have been to allocate the estimated $400,000 compensation expense (100,000 options × $4 estimated option value at date of grant) over the employment period required for the options to vest. Realistically, the firm's accountants should reduce estimated option value below $4 to reflect liquidity and forfeiture considerations identified earlier.

To their credit, standard setters would not let go of the option valuation issue. In 1984 the FASB added stock option accounting to its agenda and studied the issue for nine years. Its June 1993 Exposure Draft concluded that options have measurable value beyond the difference between market and exercise price on grant date. This sum should be charged to expense over an appropriate vesting period.

The FASB hit a nerve and received 1,786 comment letters. Technology firms worried that lower reported earnings would depress stock prices. Employees feared their companies, when forced to record a charge to earnings for option grants, would hesitate to distribute future awards. Recently hired workers would not share the windfall enjoyed by the Class of 1986. The FASB held six days of public hearings in Connecticut and California.

On March 25, 1994, three thousand people met at the San Jose Convention Center to protest the accounting proposal.

California treasurer and gubernatorial candidate Kathleen Brown urged lawmakers to give stock a chance and protect California's engine of economic growth. One pundit called this meeting the first mass rally against an accounting standard.[10] A nonbinding U.S. Senate resolution stated the FASB "should not at this time change the current generally accepted accounting treatment of stock options."[11]

Finally, in October 1995, after roundtable discussions and further meetings, the FASB issued Statement 123, *Accounting for Stock-Based Compensation.* Paragraph 60 acknowledged that the debate on stock option accounting "became so divisive that it threatened the Board's future working relationship with some of its constituents." The Statement offered a compromise.

Statement 123 stated unequivocally that options have value that can be estimated by formal option pricing models. However, the Statement allowed companies a choice of between (1) expensing estimated option values over employee service periods and (2) accounting for options in the manner offered by Opinion 25 with disclosure of pro forma earnings had the options been valued and expensed under the preferred fair value method.

The FASB allowed the disclosure alternative to bring closure to the debate, not because it believed that solution was the best way to improve financial reporting. Arthur Levitt later admitted that urging the FASB to back off from its proposal to expense options was "the biggest mistake I made" as SEC chairman.[12]

As of 2001, 99 percent of the Fortune 500 used employee stock options.[13] Only Boeing and grocer Winn-Dixie expensed stock option compensation on the income statement. Sadly, Boeing became mired in contract and sex scandals and Winn-Dixie subsequently declared bankruptcy. Pristine financial accounting provides no guarantee of business success.

In the wake of the accounting scandals emerging since 2001, over 750 public companies voluntarily adopted or announced intention to adopt the fair-value accounting method. The London-based International Accounting Standards Board had issued

International Financial Reporting Standard 2 the previous February, requiring that option awards be expensed.

In December 2004, the FASB summoned the will to close this chapter with issuance of Statement 123R (revised), *Share-Based Payment.* The Board required companies to value option grants with pricing models and charge this sum to earnings over appropriate service periods. Statement 123R was an important step in the formal harmonization of international accounting standards.

The case study of options accounting shows management's continued preoccupation with reported earnings and disdain for economic research. Beginning in 1992 the SEC required firms to disclose option awards and expiration dates in proxy statements. This disclosure allowed researchers to infer dates of companies' annual option award cycles. Evidence suggested that management teams timed financial disclosure around stock award dates to manage investor expectations.

Unfavorable financial disclosures came before awards, which, a cynic could argue, depresses stock prices and increases the number of options granted for a given dollar value of variable compensation. Good news came to be disclosed after awards to prevent a run-up in the stock price and reduction in the number of options granted for a fixed dollar award.[14]

When offered academic evidence at an FASB hearing that stock markets shrug off accounting adjustments, the Home Depot chairman snapped, "You're trying to confuse me with logic here. It's not going to work. I deal with the emotional side of the street. I deal with Wall Street."[15] No amount of science could convince this manager that financial markets are reasonably efficient.

Two researchers conducted a study of 54 companies to see what happened to stock prices after announcement that options would be expensed in 2002 and 2003. The accounting change was expected to reduce average earnings per share (EPS) by 13 percent. In an earlier survey of professors, 86 percent thought the accounting change would not affect company stock prices.

The researchers confirmed academic intuition. There was no significant consequence of expensing options on company stock prices. Further, there was an absence of correlation between individual company share price changes and the magnitude of EPS decreases.[16] The study's results were consistent with University of Chicago studies that markets see through accounting window dressing when valuing securities.

In 2005 Internet technology provider Cisco Systems, a big options user, teamed with investment bank Morgan Stanley to address perceived shortfalls in option valuation models. They proposed to invite 15 disinterested institutional money managers to bid on a modest offering of warrants that matched Cisco's employee option grants. The securities would have the same exercise price, vesting schedule, restrictions on trading and hedging, and settlement in shares. The market bids would form the basis for an observable market price to reliably quantify compensation cost.

The 1980s' use of debt showed problems with sticks. The 1990s' use of options showed problems with carrots. No one has found a simple solution for measuring option costs. Problems with obtaining agreement on valuation, and consequent actions of users of options as a compensation tool, illustrate the political nature of financial accounting standard setting.

13

EARNINGS

The simplest, most visible, most merciless measure of corporate success in the 1990s has become this one: Did you make your earnings last quarter?

—Justin Fox, *Fortune*, March 31, 1997

Previous chapters showed how statement preparers did not pay much attention to the efficient markets hypothesis, capital asset pricing model, and Black-Scholes option valuation model. Some management teams thus believed that (1) investors could be fooled by financial statement presentation, (2) reporting volatile earnings was a sign of weakness, and (3) option awards had little cost.

The rise of firms that aggregate earnings forecasts elevated the importance of consensus earnings. Management at many companies became obsessed with using accounting tools to meet quarterly targets and thus boost stock prices to inflate the value of option awards.

➤

Financial statement users assess firms' ability to repay debt or declare dividends. These distributions require cash. The income statement becomes the inevitable starting point for such evaluation. Excess of revenues over expenses provides a measure of cash a firm should realize from transactions reported in an accounting period. The trick is determining which historical activities can be expected to recur or grow in the future. Projecting earnings constitutes the core of credit and equity analysis.

Accountants struggle to define earnings and income, words used interchangeably in this chapter. These terms measure net inflows increasing wealth. A crude analogy is a bathtub where the water level represents wealth at a point in time. The spout's inflows constitute revenues and gains; the drain's outflows represent expenses and losses. Related rates determine the water level's change over an accounting period. Income is the amount of water that could be removed this period without depleting the initial water level.

Earnings represent the single most important item in corporate financial reports. Over a one-to-ten-year horizon, stock returns appear to be explained overwhelmingly by a firm's cumulative earnings during the period. The explanatory power of other possible metrics like dividends, cash flows, and capital expenditures pales in comparison.[1] Equity investors buy securities for prospects of future earnings.

Almost every stock investor turns to the most recent income statement as the stepping-off point to project corporate earnings. These financial statement readers parse earnings into separate categories to evaluate earnings power. Table 13.1 shows a useful framework suggested by a leading accounting textbook.

Earnings likely to recur and grow garner the most respect. Investors award the highest importance to the presence or absence of operating income from sale of core products and services. Investors give less credit for recurring income from peripheral activities in the lower left-hand quadrant, even though some firms stumbled into the leasing business and eventually made more money from financing than from manufactur-

Table 13.1   Decomposition of Income to Assess Earnings Power

	Recurring	*Nonrecurring*
Primary	Operating profit from sale of core products	Profit from discontinued product lines
Peripheral	Interest income on excess cash holdings	Insurance proceeds from a building damaged by fire

Source: Inspired by Stickney and Weil, p. 687.

ing. They give little or no future credit for income appearing in the right-hand quadrants.

Management teams often classify revenues and expenses to influence analyst views of future earnings capacity. Corporate reports often break out bad news as one-time or nonrecurring expenses to suggest that future revenue will not be burdened with like charges. In 1989 Exxon showed the *Valdez* oil spill cleanup costs as a separate line item on its income statement.[2] Unusual or one-off income gains (e.g., profit from an asset sale or a favorable litigation settlement) may not receive similar treatment.

Accounting standard setters recognized early on the importance investors attach to recurring and nonrecurring income. The Committee on Accounting Procedure issued Bulletin 32, *Income and Earned Surplus,* in December 1947 to recommend classification criteria to make income statements more useful. An important objective of income presentation was "avoidance of any practice that leads to income equalization,"[3] a term I interpret as smoothing. Presumably outsiders want to see unvarnished income figures to assess a company's earnings power.

The Committee sought to distinguish operating income and charges from nonoperating gains and losses. Operating items tend to be recurring, dependable, and a normal part of a company's affairs, whereas nonoperating items are considered to be irregular, unpredictable, fortuitous, or accidental. Bulletin 32 permitted two approaches for reporting nonoperating items: show them separately in the income statement or bypass the income statement and post them as changes in shareholders' equity.

Interestingly, CAP warned the accounting community that well-informed persons often attach undue importance to earnings per share (EPS) numbers reported in newspapers, investors' services, and annual reports. If calculation of net income included material, extraordinary charges or credits, then CAP strongly encouraged management to break out the per share consequence of these items when presenting EPS.

Over the next 20 years newspapers, analyst write-ups, and corporate reports reached ever-larger audiences. Such reporting often came in highly condensed form. A public policy concern was whether investors and creditors would be drawn to potentially misleading bottom-line figures. This issue was one of classification, not recognition or valuation.

The successor Accounting Principles Board attacked this problem vigorously, issuing a number of Opinions, presented in Table 13.2, on how to classify earnings.

The APB pushed firms to report nonrecurring items net of taxes as separate line items on the income statement. Only in rare circumstances, opined the APB, should gains or losses bypass the income statement to be recorded as an adjustment to beginning-of-period retained earnings.

Table 13.2 APB Opinions for Classifying Reported Earnings

Opinion	Issue Date	Topic
9	December 1966	Extraordinary Items, Prior Period Adjustments, Earnings per Share
15	May 1969	Earnings per Share
20	July 1971	Accounting Changes
28	May 1973	Interim Financial Reporting
30	June 1973	Segment Disposal; Extraordinary, Unusual, and Infrequent Transactions

➤

To make earnings figures comparable across firms, accountants and analysts divide corporate income by a firm's number of shares outstanding to compute EPS. The ratio of stock price to EPS allows analysts to gauge investor sentiment for earnings growth: higher ratios suggest greater market enthusiasm for a firm's prospects.

Some firms had long reported EPS as a supplementary measure. Issuance of Opinion 9 in 1966 represented a first pass at prescribing how to measure this figure. It remains the only instance where GAAP specifies how to calculate a ratio.[4] GAAP focuses on earnings, not cash. Paragraph 33 of Statement 95 prohibits reporting cash flow per share.[5]

At least three problems complicate EPS calculation. Income in the numerator is a flow value, whereas the number of shares in the denominator is a stock value at a point in time. Second, income figures often include peripheral and nonrecurring activities. Finally, corporations sometimes issue debt and preferred stock that could eventually be converted into common stock. The presence of securities with embedded stock options confounds determination of the number of shares outstanding.

Accounting standard setters developed arbitrary rules to cope with these measurement problems. Messiness aside, EPS emerged as the ultimate financial reporting sound bite, able to reduce the financial consequences of a corporation's actions over a 90-day period to a single number.

It is difficult to overstate EPS's importance within the investing community. At a lunch in the early 1960s a colleague from a rival firm asked a Price Waterhouse technical partner, "Don't you think it's really our job to help our clients get the highest possible earnings per share?"[6] Tenneco's CEO reported in the 1994 annual report that the goal of delivering consistent increases in earnings guided decision making. That same year Bank of America's CEO commented that increasing EPS was the firm's most important objective. Enron's 2000 annual report letter to shareholders promised the firm was "laser-focused" on earnings per share.

Earning per share figures mean little in isolation. Users need reference points to assess whether recent figures represent good or bad news. The three most commonly used benchmarks are zero (i.e., did the firm post a profit or a loss?); EPS for the same quarter last year (did the firm post annual growth in quarterly earnings?); and consensus EPS estimates (did the firm beat the average estimate of Wall Street analysts covering the firm?).

In 1970 securities broker Lynch, Jones & Ryan began collecting profit estimates made by analysts at other firms. Two years later Lynch published the average estimate for 600 companies in a monthly newsletter called the Institutional Brokers Estimates System (I/B/E/S). In 1978 Chicago analyst Leonard Zacks founded Zacks Investment Research. Other firms followed suit. In 1984 nine brokerage firms teamed up to create First Call.[7]

Such aggregators calculated earnings surprises, the difference between reported EPS and the estimate average. By the late 1980s these firms distributed results electronically to a wide audience. *Making* earnings became a measure of success; *missing* earnings was a sign of weakness. There can be little doubt aggregators influenced corporate reporting behavior. A 1994 Merrill Lynch study showed more than half of money managers surveyed used earnings surprises and earnings estimate revisions when making investment decisions.[8]

Microsoft, on its way to becoming the most world's valuable company, reported earnings that met or beat Wall Street estimates in 41 of the 42 quarters ending December 1996. It is unlikely to be a coincidence that seven of the top 10 1997 *Fortune* most admired rankings missed fewer than five quarters in the previous five years.[9] Unbiased earnings estimates would result in favorable variances only half the time.

The ultimate measure of corporate success in the 1990s was producing a long, consistent earnings trajectory. Rational managers, trying to impress outside observers, tried to routinely meet or beat the consensus number by a small amount. Earnings coming in well above a threshold would simply cause outsiders to raise the bar further, making management's job that much more difficult in the next year. Executives would adjust accruals (e.g., reduce the estimate for bad debt expense) to raise earnings in the face of a shortfall.

Earnings management became the art of recognizing gains and losses in a necessary fashion to smooth out bumps and avoid a decline.[10] Figure 13.1 shows a stylized example.

All businesses mature. None can grow faster in perpetuity than the U.S. economy; otherwise that firm becomes the U.S. economy. Corporations that choose to smooth earnings can get into trouble toward the end of the business life cycle. Management must come up with increasingly heroic assumptions to meet ever higher earnings targets extrapolated from a linear trend.

CEOs faced increasing pressure to boost stock prices in the early 1990s. Boards sacked IBM's John Akers, Westinghouse's Paul Lego, American Express's James D. Robinson, and General

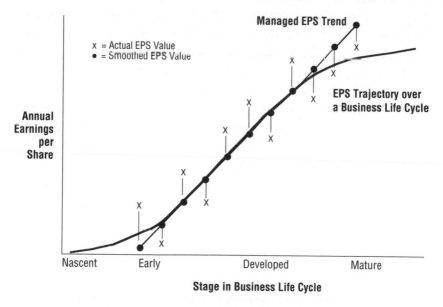

Figure 13.1   Stylized Example of Smoothing Earnings

Motors' Robert Stempel for lagging stock performance.[11] The SEC may have aggravated the problem by requiring public companies to publish a stock return chart in proxy statements detailing five-year performance relative to an industry peer group and a broader market index.

Extreme pressure to produce earnings growth was a 1990s phenomenon. Managers in the 1920s, working at the time of the previous great stock bubble, felt no such pressure. Contemporary investors did not demand steady year-to-year earnings increases. Rising managers received less frequent promotions or transfers. Executives came from technical and manufacturing ranks and turned to operations, not accounting, to create wealth.[12]

Time series studies of earnings released from the 1947 through 1966 suggested that period-to-period movement in earnings was random even though earnings-based executive compensation emerged in the 1950s.[13] A General Motors financial reporting executive writing in 1983 felt that government and media charges of earnings management were vastly overrated.[14]

The tone changed in the 1990s with the success of blue-chip firms such as General Electric. CEO Jack Welch assembled a series of managers and businesses that created one of the great success stories of modern business. Table 13.3 presents GE's extraordinary earnings trend.

Wall Street approved of this amazing trajectory and rewarded GE with increasing price-earnings (P/E) ratios over the decade. Compounding effects of higher earnings and P/E multiple expansion propelled GE's share valuation into the stratosphere. The firm reached the top of *Fortune*'s most admired corporation list in 1998. Yet some analysts questioned GE's unerring ability to meet quarterly earnings numbers in the face of global political, currency, and economic risks. Critics suggested GE managed earnings by timing the recognition of gains and losses to artificially smooth its earnings path.

"We manage businesses, not earnings," intoned GE's 2001 an-

**Table 13.3   Consistent Earnings Growth
Brought GE Enhanced Market Valuation**

Year	Diluted EPS	P/E Ratio	Year-End Stock Price	Indexed Value	
				GE	S&P 500
1990	$0.40	12.0	$ 4.78	100	100
1991	0.25	25.5	6.38	133	126
1992	0.49	14.5	7.13	149	132
1993	0.42	20.8	8.74	183	141
1994	0.58	14.7	8.50	178	139
1995	0.65	18.5	12.00	251	187
1996	0.73	22.6	16.48	345	224
1997	0.83	29.5	24.46	512	294
1998	0.95	35.8	34.00	711	372
1999	1.09	47.3	51.58	1,079	445
2000	1.29	37.2	47.94	1,003	400

Source: Computed from data in company annual reports and Yahoo! Finance.

nual report letter to shareholders. An anecdote from Welch's autobiography belies this claim. In April 1994 he learned a Kidder Peabody trader's position created the need to record an unfavorable $350 million accounting adjustment. Welch explains:

> The response of our business leaders to the crisis was typical of the GE culture. Even though the books had closed on the quarter, many immediately offered to pitch in to cover the Kidder gap. Some said they could find an extra $10 million, $20 million, and even $30 million from the businesses to offset the surprise. Though it was too late, their willingness to help was a dramatic contrast to the excuses I had been hearing from the Kidder people.[15]

Management teams sought to emulate GE's success. The widespread use of option compensation plans compounded the issue. Since options represent leveraged investments, small changes in stock prices can cause disproportionate changes in option values. Managers with sizable option grants could become extremely sensitive to stock price changes. Two researchers found that managers paid comparatively high levels of stock compensation were more likely to report earnings that met or just beat analysts' forecasts compared to managers paid with low equity incentives.[16]

Academics found overwhelming evidence that companies manage earnings to avoid decreases or losses. Firms reporting a pattern of consistently higher earnings enjoyed higher stock market valuations. Further, the premium grew as the series continued for longer periods of time.[17] Firms that habitually met or beat earnings estimates enjoyed higher stock market returns than firms that failed to meet expectations. This valuation premium carried over to firms that openly engaged in earnings and expectations management.[18]

With the rise of aggregators reporting consensus estimates and earnings surprises, EPS became a ridiculously important measure of corporate performance. A majority of 400 executives surveyed by three professors admitted they would delay maintenance or advertising expenditures—or even give up good investments—to smooth reported EPS because stock market reactions to an earnings miss became so significant.[19]

Making accounting adjustments to offset economic, political, and business risks so that reported EPS beat consensus numbers by a penny was tantamount, as one executive described, to landing a 747 on a postage stamp.

How could a penny a share matter? Investors believed well-run companies could always find a penny or two per share. Small misses offered evidence of hidden problems. This cockroach theory held that revealing one small problem suggested the presence of hundreds more behind the wall. Missing a number implied management had little control over the firm.

The problem got worse as the decade progressed. Some believed short sellers, who benefit from falling stock prices, exploited the importance of EPS by planting artificially high whisper earnings numbers to ensure the company failed to meet inflated estimates.

Financial professionals facilitating smooth earnings growth became rock stars in the business press. *CFO* magazine's annual excellence awards cited WorldCom's Scott Sullivan in 1998, Enron's Andrew Fastow in 1999, and Tyco's Mark Swartz in 2000.[20] The federal government would indict all three.

On Monday, September 28, 1998, SEC Chairman Arthur Levitt gave the most significant speech in the history of U.S. accounting. In a presentation at New York University, birthplace of modern accounting education, he railed against the "numbers game," a too-little-challenged custom where management suppressed commonsense business practices, satisfied consensus earnings estimates, and projected a smooth earnings path in an attempt to grow a company's stock price and the value of underlying options. Misuse of reserves, special charges, and other trickery served to obscure actual financial volatility.[21]

Levitt recognized the penalty for a company failing to make its numbers. He cited a Fortune 500 firm that missed consensus earnings by a penny and then lost 6 percent of its market value. The solution, he believed, was increased disclosure. In the face of opaque earnings, investors panicked as a result of unexpected or unquantifiable bad news.

The EPS bubble burst when accounting scandals came to light at the turn of the millennium. According to research from Thomson First Call, in 1998 stock prices of the 30 companies in the Dow Jones Industrial Average that beat consensus estimates by a penny saw a stock price increase of 0.78 percent on the day of the announcement; by 2004, the effect diminished to 0.15 percent.[22]

Further evidence that EPS has lost its luster comes from a survey of the number of times "earnings per share" and "earnings estimate" appeared in *Wall Street Journal* articles, as documented in Figure 13.2.

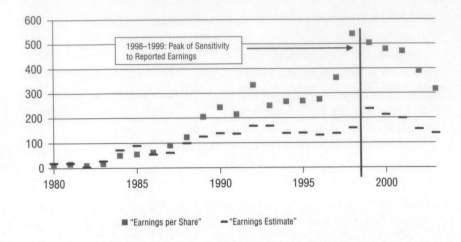

■ "Earnings per Share"   — "Earnings Estimate"

	[1]	[2]		[1]	[2]
1980	9	19	1992	333	167
1981	15	19	1993	250	168
1982	10	3	1994	266	138
1983	16	27	1995	268	139
1984	49	71	1996	275	130
1985	55	89	1997	362	137
1986	61	54	1998	541	159
1987	90	60	1999	504	237
1988	123	98	2000	479	212
1989	205	125	2001	470	198
1990	243	138	2002	390	154
1991	215	136	2003	316	138

Number of articles appearing in the *Wall Street Journal* using the words:
[1] "EPS" or "earnings per share"
[2] "Earnings estimate"

Figure 13.2   Annual Counts of *Wall Street Journal* Articles Using Phrases Associated with Earnings
Source: Factiva.

The incidence of these phrases and the importance attached to reported earnings diminished with the wave of accounting scandals. One observer made the following assessment in 2003:

> In fact, what seems to have been occurring was a game in which analysts and investors were testing the quality of a company's stated earnings by determining whether management could hit its targets. If it could, that meant that the company's earnings were probably growing, although not necessarily as stated. If it could not, the company had apparently run out of ways to improve its results, suggesting that its earnings had fallen dramatically. This odd game of inferences created the strange market phenomenon in which companies that missed their earnings by a penny or two saw 20% or 30% declines in their share prices.
>
> The problem isn't the earnings game. It's that profitability in GAAP terms is largely an estimate. Excessive reliance on GAAP thus does more harm than good. The real cure should have been changes in the securities laws and enforcement so that other kinds of financial and non-financial disclosure could gain traction.[23]

Reported earnings became important because management actions made them so important.

A parallel story to this EPS drama was rise of pro forma earnings. "For the sake of form" in Latin, this term applies to disclosures designed to present data for hypothetical situations such as proposed mergers or implications of alternate accounting treatment.

Technology firms in the 1990s issued press releases featuring pro forma earnings figures in addition to earnings prepared under GAAP. The most common adjustments excluded amortization of goodwill and other intangible assets, stock-based compensation expenses, and costs associated with acquisitions. Pro forma earnings during this period were invariably higher than those reported under GAAP.[24]

Telecom companies' enormous infrastructure investments saddled earnings with large depreciation charges. One way to burnish reported performance was to focus investor attention on earnings before interest, taxes, depreciation, and amortization (EBITDA). Warren Buffett poked fun at this practice by asking if the tooth fairy bore responsibility for making capital expenditures.

Advocates argued that pro forma figures presented more meaningful accounting information; critics charged that this tool obscured economic performance. Earnings press releases, with pro forma figures, issued before formal SEC filings did not fall under GAAP's jurisdiction.

Qwest Communications' financial reporting for the year ending December 31, 2000, illustrates this issue. Qwest issued its earnings release for the fourth quarter of 2000 on January 24, 2001, the date Arthur Andersen gave a clean audit opinion. The body of the release did not cite a GAAP net income figure. Instead, the release provided figures on "a pro forma normalized basis and excluding non-recurring items." Full-year 2000 pro forma EPS of $0.59 grew 51 percent from the $0.39 reported for 1999. One could infer Qwest had had a great year.

Then, on March 16, 2001, Qwest filed its annual Form 10-K with the SEC. The GAAP income statement showed diluted earnings per share dropped from $1.52 in 1999 to –$0.06 in 2000. Qwest's GAAP earnings didn't grow by half; they evaporated. Outrage over such practices prompted the SEC to issue Regulation G in March 2003 to require registrants to reconcile pro forma earnings figures to balances calculated under GAAP.

However, it's not clear that use of EBITDA and pro forma figures hurt the investing public. Two researchers compared stock prices and earnings data for companies that did and did not report pro forma numbers. They found little difference in stock price behavior. In other words, investors did not appear to price shares of firms issuing pro forma earnings differently from those disclosing only GAAP numbers.[25]

➤

Perhaps management's objective in selection of financial accounting policies is to minimize cost of equity capital. Predictable earnings may satisfy investor wants and reduce returns they require. Reduced equity costs make future earnings more attractive and raise a firm's stock price. Four researchers estimated how companies' cost of equity varied with the presence or absence of seven seemingly desirable traits of reported earnings. Earnings quality (absence of managed accruals) trumped all other attributes, including predictability and smoothness.[26]

Investors recognize that recording unfavorable accruals does not cause cancer. Statement 106, *Employers' Accounting for Postretirement Benefits Other Than Pensions,* issued December 1990, required employers to stop recording retiree health care expenses on a cash, pay-as-you-go basis. Employers had to start accruing for these employee benefits as earned. IBM adopted the standard in March 1991, sustaining a $2.3 billion charge and a notable event, its first-ever quarterly loss.[27] Investors shrugged off the accrual, and no one agitated for the firm to abandon its health care plans.

14

SOX

I am not an accountant.

—Enron's Jeffrey Skilling in
congressional testimony

The train wreck started on October 12, 2001. An Andersen attorney sent an e-mail to the Houston office about the firm's document retention policy. Four days later Enron released third quarter earnings figures and disclosed several asset write-downs. Traders and creditors lost confidence in Enron's ability to honor obligations. On December 2 the firm declared bankruptcy with $63 billion in assets, the largest in U.S. history based on this measure.

On January 28, 2002, Global Crossing declared bankruptcy with $30 billion in total assets, the fourth largest to that time. On July 21, WorldCom declared bankruptcy with $104 billion in assets.[1] Legislators enacted the Sarbanes-Oxley Act on July 30. Andersen had given unqualified audit opinions to all three firms, received a criminal indictment, and shut its doors to new business on August 31.

Financial reporting's annus horribilis witnessed three of the five largest U.S. bankruptcies, passage of the most invasive security legislation since the Depression, and dissolution of what had once been the world's leading CPA firm. Bad accounting played little role in the 1929 Crash but was at the heart of this disaster.

U.S. financial accounting history since the Depression has been about efforts to reduce diversity of practice. Anticipated benefits included improved quality of accounts, increased understanding of company disclosure, and enhanced comparisons across companies. Cumulative efforts of the Committee on Accounting Procedure (CAP), Accounting Principles Board (APB), and Financial Accounting Standards Board (FASB) made progress. However, experience with investment tax credits, oil exploration, debt restructurings, and stock options showed politics hobble the standard-setting process.

London Business School professor William Baxter, speaking in 1979, joked that in a world made safe by enough standards, accounting would be plagued by few scandals. Noisy defamers would have to hunt elsewhere for quarry. Kidding aside, he held a dim view of increased reliance on formal rules. What start out as gentle guides become bright-line rules backed by sanctions. Judgment yields to petrified procedures. Standards, he prophesied, bring setbacks and disillusion.[2]

Not everyone shared Baxter's gloom. Speaking in November 1999, General Electric comptroller Philip Ameen acknowledged that financial reporting could be improved but felt that nothing he'd seen suggested the United States was experiencing even a 1 percent rate of material error in financial information.[3]

In May 2001, four months before the Enron scandal, SEC chief accountant Lynn Turner gave a speech on the state of financial reporting. He said that investor confidence was at an all-time high (84 million Americans, 44 percent of the adult population, owned equities as of 1998), due in part to improvements in financial reporting made over the preceding 25 years.

Contributions cited included the Cohen Commission on auditing and creation of the Public Oversight Board (1977), Treadway Commission on internal controls (1987), Special Report of the Public Oversight Board (1994), U.S. General Accounting Officer report on the accounting profession (1996), New York Stock Exchange Blue Ribbon Panel on Audit Committees (1999), and O'Malley Panel on audit effectiveness (2000).

"Because of these accomplishments, I do believe that the transparency and quality of financial reporting today is better than what it was 25, or even 10, years ago," Turner said.[4] He did not comment on some companies' pathological fear of reporting debt on balance sheets or volatile earnings on income statements.

In 1985 economist Kenneth Lay orchestrated the merger of Houston Natural Gas and InterNorth to create a debt-laden natural gas pipeline company. The firm changed its name to Enron and promoted aggressive Harvard MBAs Rebecca Mark and Jeffrey Skilling. Mark developed large overseas utility projects while Skilling created a natural gas trading desk that expanded into electricity and other commodities. Asset-intensive projects plus a vibrant trading operation created a voracious appetite for new capital. In August 2000 Enron's stock price peaked at $91 ($66 billion market capitalization); within five quarters, the firm would be bankrupt.

The firm's managers identified two accounting tools to burnish reported results and make Enron securities appear more attractive to investors and creditors. Management embraced the trading classification of securities offered by Statement 115. Almost every company shies away from volatile marked-to-market adjustments that flow noisy holding gains and losses through the income statement. Enron saw this treatment as an opportunity to report attractive results.

Statement 115 contemplated reference to liquid capital markets when marking securities to market quotes. Enron's arcane contracts and illiquid securities lacked deep markets. Instead of looking up prices in news service databases, Enron used financial models to value positions. Its *mark-to-model* system allowed traders to influence valuation decisions.

Accountants had no reference points to challenge traders' marks. Modest adjustments to valuation models could increase a position's alleged value and cause an offsetting credit to flow through Enron's income statement. Reporting ephemeral unrealized holding gains could support a smooth earnings trajectory.

It was a lot easier to manipulate assumptions in a computer model than change the asset's historical cost. At December 31, 2000, Enron assigned a fair value of $125 million to its interest in a joint venture and posted a $53 million boost to reported earnings even though the entity had not recognized any revenue.[5] In 2000, more than half of Enron's reported profits came from mark-to-market adjustment gains.[6]

Second, Enron exploited a quirk in consolidation accounting rules to make extensive use of the special purpose entity (SPE). Corporations had long used SPEs to carry out specific activities that required creation of a bankruptcy-remote subsidiary. Typically a sponsoring corporation creates an SPE to support an asset transfer, such as sale of receivables. The SPE borrows money from third parties, uses proceeds to buy assets from the selling corporation, and offers divisible interests to investors. Such SPEs ensure investors receive promised cash flows in the event of financial distress suffered by sponsors.

A series of arcane FASB Emerging Issues Task Force releases permitted sponsors to avoid consolidating SPEs when outsiders provided equity financing amounting to at least 3 percent of the entity's assets.[7] A firm seeking to transfer $100 million of assets to an unconsolidated SPE would need to arrange for outsiders to put up just $3 million of equity.

Unconsolidated SPEs deemed outside Enron's control offered two benefits. The SPEs could borrow lots of money yet the debt would not appear on Enron's balance sheet. Further, Enron could sell assets to these entities at inflated prices and record realized gains on the income statement.

Chief financial officer Andrew Fastow stretched the 3 percent rule and oversaw a Byzantine network of perhaps 3,500 SPEs[8] under management control. The entities provided Enron the opportunity to fabricate earnings and engage in massive off-balance-sheet borrowing. Enron simply borrowed more than could be supported by operating cash flows. Where were the auditors? The 2000 proxy showed that Andersen received $25 million in auditing fees and $27 million in consulting revenue. One questions Andersen partners' fervor to challenge Enron management and risk losing a $50 million account.

The party came to an end on October 16, 2001, when Enron's quarterly earnings release described a billion-dollar charge to write down inflated investments. Under nonrecurring items, management cited a $287 million asset impairment, a $180 million restructuring charge, and $544 million in investment losses including "certain structured finance arrangements with a previously disclosed entity."

A bungled conference call and series of incendiary newspaper articles followed. Enron submitted restated financial statements to the SEC on November 8. Moody's Investors Service and Standard & Poor's downgraded Enron's debt to junk status on November 28. Trading operations dried up because counterparties grew wary that Enron could not honor settlement obligations. The share price dropped below a dollar. Enron filed for bankruptcy on December 2.

Investors and creditors lost billions. Thousands of employees who invested in company stock lost not only their jobs but also their retirement savings. Accounting practices, just numbers on paper, ruined lives. Events of September 11, the anthrax scare, and war in Afghanistan overshadowed media coverage of Enron's problems. Complexities of mark-to-market accounting and consolidations likely diminished public interest. Unfortunately, the train wreck had just started.

➤

In 1972 furniture salesman Gary Winnick began selling bonds for the investment bank that would become Drexel Burnham Lambert. In 1978 he moved to Los Angeles to spend the next seven years working for junk-bond czar Michael Milken.[9] Winnick founded Pacific Capital Group in 1985 to manage money and invest in new ventures. Significant Internet growth prompted him to arrange financing for an undersea fiber-optic cable from the United States to Europe.

The project cascaded to similar ventures that were later combined to create Global Crossing, formed in March 1997 in Bermuda, a jurisdiction that allows corporations to minimize U.S. taxes on income generated in foreign jurisdictions. Winnick became chairman.

Global Crossing sought to become the world's first independent global provider of Internet and long-distance telecommunications services using a high-capacity terrestrial and undersea digital fiber-optic cable system. These collections of thin glass strands, using light pulses to carry substantially more data than could be conveyed by copper wire, were industry's solution to an apocryphal analysis that Internet traffic would double every hundred days.

Global Crossing grew to connect 200 of the world's largest metropolitan communications markets in Asia, Europe, and the Americas. Operations began in October 1997 and the company went public in August 1998. Global Crossing, in a position similar to that of emerging railroads, needed lots of money to continue construction of an ever-expanding network. Demand would certainly exceed supply for years to come.

Winnick stole a page from the Drexel playbook and financed construction with an alphabet soup of securities: classes A through E of common stocks, three series of mandatorily redeemable preferred stock, and a panoply of debt instruments. Pacific Capital then secured warrants, long-term options, to purchase Global

Crossing common stock. Winnick would make a killing if the stock appreciated substantially.

A land-grab mentality enshrouded the telecom bubble. Just as the Union Pacific and Central Pacific railroads felt a sense of urgency to lay track quickly, Global Crossing pushed to establish an early lead over competition, albeit without the benefit of government support.

Enormous start-up expenses and depreciation charges prevented the company from showing early profits. Interestingly, a significant accounting policy was capitalization of interest expense associated with construction in progress, the issue that caused the National Association of Cost Accountants' 1919 break with the American Institute of Certified Public Accountants (AICPA).

Management, with extensive option awards and an almost limitless future demand for long-term debt, felt substantial pressure to show favorable prospects to investors and creditors. How could management convey evidence of a strong earnings trajectory in the absence of profits?

Executives stressed the importance of EBITDA, a measure that attempts to strip out nonoperating and/or noncash charges from the net income figure. Accounting standard setters never sanctioned this measure because matching requires the income statement to consider all resources consumed to generate revenues. Someone has to pay for capital expenditures and financing costs. The 1907 Interstate Commerce Commission's accounting rules were designed to require railroads to charge income statements with an estimate for depreciation.

Global Crossing had reported the figures shown in Table 14.1 for long-term debt as of the previous three balance sheet dates plus revenues, losses applicable to common shareholders (after dividends to preferred stockholders), and EBITDA for the years then ended. Arthur Andersen had given an unqualified opinion dated February 14, 2001.

Put yourself in management's shoes in early 2001. Even though EBITDA showed a nice trajectory, frenetic growth caused debt

Table 14.1   Global Crossing's EBITDA
Trajectory ($ millions)

	1998	1999	2000
Long-term debt	$270	$4,900	$6,271
Revenue	424	1,491	3,789
Loss	(135)	(178)	(1,980)
EBITDA	364	626	1,469

and losses to grow quickly. How much was this venture worth? The stock market's early assessment was favorable. Global Crossing went public at $9.50 and peaked at $64.25 in the second quarter of 1999, a year before the technology bubble burst (the NASDAQ Composite index peaked on March 10, 2000, and the S&P 500 peaked two weeks later).

However, Global Crossing's customer demand dropped as competitors installed their own fiber-optic networks. The stock fell to $16.19 per share in March 2001. Management had no ability to post a profit in 2001.

A solution to further burnish results was to engage in *concurrent transactions,* otherwise known as capacity swaps. Global Crossing and competitor Qwest agreed to simultaneously purchase unused capacity from each other's network. Global Crossing recorded the nonmonetary exchanges as deferred revenue to be flowed through its income statement over the lives of the contracts. The company sought inflated revenue to give creditors the impression that revenue growth foretold future earnings: we've built it and they will come. Andersen had approved this treatment and published a white paper on accounting principles relating to exchange of telecommunications capacity.

In 1960, Leonard Spacek's Arthur Andersen published *Accounting and Reporting Problems of the Accounting Profession,* a booklet written to help partners and managers work with clients to develop sound accounting standards. One topic selected, gross sales, defined revenue in part as performance of services.[10]

Somehow Spacek's firm evolved so that it could define capacity swaps as performance of a service. In August 2001 a former Global Crossing employee complained about this treatment, and the board of directors formed a committee to study the issue.

It was too late. Cash flow did not grow fast enough to service obligations from more than $12 billion in debt. Global Crossing declared bankruptcy on January 28, 2002. In August the SEC communicated to the AICPA its displeasure with Global Crossing's recording of revenue in connection with capacity swaps.

In October Global Crossing announced plans to restate 2000's financial statements and retained Grant Thornton as new auditors. Winnick resigned in December. Qwest, the swaps counterparty and another Andersen client, also announced it would restate earnings.

In September 2002 hearings of the U.S. House Committee on Energy and Commerce's Subcommittee on Oversight and Investigations, Representative Billy Tauzin railed against a "number-obsessed atmosphere" where Global Crossing management constructed sham transactions to meet publicly announced revenue targets.[11]

In December 2003, Global Crossing filed a Form 10-K for 2002 and emerged from bankruptcy. Remarkably, its fourth quarter 2002 results showed a $24.9 billion profit, the highest quarterly net income that had ever been registered by a U.S. company.[12] Eight billion dollars of gain came from elimination of liabilities and 16 billion from elimination of all common and preferred shares outstanding. Some 13,000 people lost their jobs, Andersen received a second black eye, and Global Crossing stock resumed trading on the NASDAQ as a slimmed-down organization.

In 1983 one-time milkman and high school basketball coach Bernie Ebbers invested in reseller Long-Distance Discount Service and became CEO two years later. An improbable string of mergers and acquisitions, capped by a 1997 $37 billion deal with

MCI, transformed the scrappy firm into WorldCom, a major player in the U.S. telecommunications market.

Ebbers became a billionaire. Loath to sell shares, he borrowed money secured by WorldCom stock to pay for a yacht company, rice farm, and elevated lifestyle. Stock price declines could trigger margin calls or unwanted sale of collateral. Resulting fixation with share price led Ebbers to pester his CFO over intraday movements and harangue executives who sold stock.[13]

WorldCom peaked at $64 in the second quarter of 1999. Prospects then headed south after a failed bid for rival Sprint, the tech crash, and a softening economy. By the third quarter of 2000 the stock traded as low as $25 and Ebbers demanded that the company hit unreasonable earnings targets to restore shares to former glory.[14]

The firm had reported losses in 1996 and 1998. WorldCom wrote off acquired in-process research and development costs amounting, respectively, to nearly 10 percent and 18 percent of revenues. Management likely engaged in spring-loading to give greater assurance of reporting future earnings growth.

Most promising were declining line costs. These access charges reflect use of others' network infrastructures. As presented in Table 14.2, WorldCom showed a beautiful trajectory of margin improvement through 2000. The bursting of the telecom bubble plus a soft economy in the wake of 9/11 caused a revenue reduction and margin setback in 2001, a reasonable result because some line costs did not vary directly with revenue volume.

Yet not all was as it seemed. WorldCom began making accounting adjustments in late 2000 to capitalize line costs, classifying them as property, plant, and equipment. An untrained

Table 14.2   WorldCom's Line Cost Trajectory

	1997	1998	1999	2000	2001
Revenues ($ millions)	7,384	17,617	35,908	39,090	35,179
Line costs ($ millions)	3,764	7,982	14,739	15,462	14,739
Percent of revenues	51.0%	45.3%	41.0%	39.6%	41.9%

accountant could be forgiven for ill-conceived SPE or capacity swap journal entries; this blunder of capitalizing line costs defies explanation because even the most junior accountant could not make such a mistake.

In its 2000 10-K filing, management had attributed reduced line costs to changes in product mix plus scale economies achieved through skilled assimilation of acquisitions. In other words, WorldCom cited business acumen as the reason for increasing profitability.

Rival AT&T simply expensed line costs and did not understand that WorldCom was playing accounting games. WorldCom's reported results made AT&T look like a lumbering giant. Under pressure, AT&T's CEO axed 20,000 jobs and spent $100 billion to acquire TCI, Media One, and other cable companies, perhaps ruining the firm.[15] WorldCom's accounting ruse, just numbers on paper, influenced AT&T decisions that affected thousands of lives.

WorldCom's CFO later testified that his boss instructed, "We have got to hit our numbers." After receiving complaints in October 2000 from accounting department employees about capitalizing line costs, he handwrote a note to Ebbers saying, "In the future, it will be up to the operations of our company to hit our earnings targets and not up to the accounting department."[16]

Another tool used to reverse sagging investor confidence was to issue a tracking stock in June 2001. Shareholders could now trade no-dividend, high-growth WorldCom shares independently from the dividend-paying MCI shares tracking the firm's slow-growth, cash-rich business. Unfortunately, tracking stocks require arbitrary cost allocation decisions to partition earnings, and directors may experience a conflict of interest over which group of investors to favor when making business decisions. The gimmickry didn't work.

WorldCom's fortunes flagged under a weakening telecom market and massive debt. Ebbers resigned on April 29, 2002. On May 15, KPMG replaced Andersen as outside auditor. On June 25 the firm announced results of an internal audit showing that the capitalization of $3.9 billion of line transfer costs was not in accordance with GAAP. The SEC filed a civil action the next day. The firm filed for bankruptcy on July 21. WorldCom made subsequent announcements on August 8 and November 5 to disclose additional line cost issues, with a cumulative estimate of problem entries amounting to $9 billion.

Management published its 2002 10-K a year late with restated balances. Two big changes were to flow improperly capitalized line costs through the income statement (2000's line costs should have amounted to 43.0 percent of revenues instead of the reported 39.6 percent) and declare that some $40 billion of goodwill and other intangible assets were impaired and should have been written off.

After reflecting all adjustments, WorldCom's reported December 31, 2001, shareholders' equity dropped from a positive $58 billion, as initially reported and audited by Arthur Andersen, to a negative $13 billion as restated and audited by KPMG. Both figures were prepared under the same accounting principles. The difference probably represents the largest misstatement in the history of accounting.

WorldCom emerged from bankruptcy under the name MCI. But once again, innocent employees lost their jobs and investors and creditors lost billions.

Also occurring in 2002 were the Adelphia Communications and Tyco International looting scandals. John Rigas had grown Adelphia from humble origins to a major cable television system and Internet service provider. However, the telecom giant retained workings of a family-owned business. Management orchestrated transactions with family-controlled businesses to siphon so much money for noncorporate projects that this healthy firm declared bankruptcy in June. A jury found Rigas guilty in 2004.

The same month that Adelphia declared bankruptcy, L. Dennis Kozlowski resigned as Tyco International's CEO. He was indicted and subsequently found guilty of grand larceny in 2005.

The money funded escapades that included a famous $6,000 shower curtain and $2 million birthday party for his wife. Most damning was evidence Kozlowski signed a personal tax return that did not report $25 million of income.[17]

The year 2002 also saw a dozen other stories of channel stuffing and barter deals designed to inflate revenue and suggest robust earnings prospects as the economy softened.

Over the past century, an expectations gap developed between CPAs and the investing public. The man on the street viewed public accountants as gatekeepers hired to identify fraudulent financial reporting. Auditing firms did little to dissuade the public's view. Yet public accountants recognized that no client would be willing to pay the enormous cost of providing audits that had a reasonable chance of identifying fraud. In fact, it was not until 1988 that the AICPA used the word *fraud* in any auditing standard.[18]

Public accountants have little hope of finding large-scale fraud. Most clients ascribed little value to the audit function and viewed the service as a commodity. Responsive auditors reduced costs by using lower-paid, recently hired college graduates to perform field work. Staff auditors in their twenties were told to work quickly to minimize billable hours. Few staffers had the street smarts and boardroom polish to identify fraud perpetrated by senior executives.

Management did not mind. While there are ready measures of audit efficiency, there are few for audit effectiveness. Given the invasive nature of audits, corporate management would just as soon select an auditing firm that charges a lower fee and renders its opinion with fewer interruptions. Investors and creditors relying on audit effectiveness do not pay for auditing services. A similar criticism has been levied against debt rating firms, whose work is paid for by bond issuers instead of the lenders who use their reports. Enron and WorldCom bonds received investment-grade ratings until just before each firm collapsed.[19]

Nevertheless, the system generally worked. Aside from some stumbles like the first McKesson fraud, the Continental Vending case, and the Penn Central bankruptcy, public accounting grew in size, stature, and wealth from the 1934 Act until the Internet bubble. Then in the late 1990s something went terribly wrong, especially at Arthur Andersen. Evidence comes from a nonscientific sample of accounting flaps, presented in Table 14.3, sorted by year and auditing firm.

The industry lost face in 2002, the year of Sarbanes-Oxley legislation and Arthur Andersen's implosion. Many public companies felt pressure to play the earnings game, and some auditors went along. Andersen seemed particularly unable to stand up to clients. Two traits distinguished the firm from competitors.

First was the power of its culture. Andersen preached conformance more strongly than other auditing firms. All new hires attended a boot camp at the Center for Professional Education in St. Charles, Illinois. The rigorous indoctrination ensured work paper documentation complied with standards established at the home office.

When I worked at Andersen from 1982 to 1985, every male professional wore a white shirt. Stripes or colors suggested the employee had an attitude problem. Professional women wore skirts and jackets, never dresses or slacks. Arthur Andersen's motto "Think Straight, Talk Straight" reminded staffers to speak literally, not figuratively, and seek direct answers instead of elegant solutions. The culture's strength was that the professional staff followed management directives swiftly and without question.

The second cause was business success of the Administrative Services Division, later known as the Management Information Consulting Division and then Andersen Consulting, an early integrator of accounting software applications. The landmark event was installing a UNIVAC computer and payroll software at GE's Appliance Park in 1953.

Managing partner Leonard Spacek advocated this project because of his work on utility audits. He understood firsthand the

Table 14.3 Significant Accounting Scandals Concentrated in 2002 among Andersen Clients

Year Scandal Broke	Arthur Andersen	Deloitte & Touche	Ernst & Young	KPMG	Pricewaterhouse Coopers
1997			Cendant		
1998	Sunbeam				McKesson
1999	Baptist Foundation Waste Management	Rite Aid			
2000				Xerox	
2001	Enron				
2002	CMS Energy Dynegy Global Crossing Halliburton Merck Peregrine Qwest WorldCom	Adelphia Duke Energy El Paso Reliant Energy		ImClone	Bristol-Myers Squibb Kmart Lucent Tyco
2003	Freddie Mac		HealthSouth		

complications of issuing invoices when a customer's rate depended on two dozen variables.[20] Increased complexity of business meant timely billing would be impossible without proper automation.

Large-scale system integration subsequently proved more profitable than commodity-like auditing services. In 1983 consulting revenue allowed Andersen to displace Peat Marwick as the largest accounting firm in the world.[21] By 1994, 46 percent of Andersen's revenues came from consulting, 16 points more than the consulting fraction of its closest peer.[22] Of Andersen's 2,134 partners in 1989, 586 (27 percent) worked in consulting but brought in 43 percent of all revenue.[23]

Resentment between old-line auditors who controlled the firm and up-and-coming consultants who brought in disproportionate profit led to a fractious divorce. In 1997 Arthur Andersen and Andersen Consulting filed suits against each other to seek a divorce in the International Court of Arbitration. Andersen Consulting, later named Accenture, spun off in 2000 under terms unfavorable to the auditors.

To seek satisfaction the auditors started a replacement consulting practice. Arthur Andersen & Co. required a sales approach, not an auditing mind-set, to pull this off quickly. The culture's strength permitted rapid adjustment.

Evidence Andersen quickly lost its way comes from the experiences of Barbara Toffler, a former Harvard Business School professor hired to bring in fee revenue selling ethics consulting services. Andersen's old guard would have sniffed that CPAs teach ethics by example instead of charging clients for the education. Dr. Toffler described the incredible pressure she felt to replace revenue lost from the Accenture spin-off. Money, not stewardship or public responsibility, was the great healer at Andersen.[24]

"To win . . . you have to break the rules," began a bizarre invitation to attend a June 27, 2000, presentation by a senior Arthur Andersen partner to members of the Cleveland business community. The line did not seem fitting for an auditing organization formed to assure financial statements comply with GAAP.

The presentation was based on *Cracking the Value Code: How Successful Businesses Are Creating Wealth in the New Economy*, a book just written by three Andersen partners, E. S. Boulton, Barry D. Libert, and Steve M. Samek. The thesis was that winning firms earn economic profit through innovative use of tangible and intangible assets. Novel business approaches can bring extraordinary riches in the New Economy.

CPAs substantiate recognition, valuation, and classification decisions made by the client's accounting staff. *Value Code*'s authors showed little interest in financial statement presentation. Instead they invested enormous effort to search for business models to help CEOs navigate the information economy. Attendees walked out thinking these guys were no longer auditors; they had become strategy consultants. CEO Joe Berardino appeared on television and said the auditor's job was "to help the client achieve its business goals."[25]

Andersen's woes began when it received a censure and record $7 million SEC fine for bungled audits of Waste Management, where the client lengthened truck depreciation lives to boost earnings. Then audit client Baptist Foundation of Arizona filed for bankruptcy in November 1999. Auditors failed to uncover a Ponzi scheme that bilked hundreds of millions of retirement savings from senior citizens. In March 2001 the firm settled and paid $217 million in damages to investors.

The next month Andersen paid a $110 million settlement to Sunbeam shareholders after failing to identify client channel stuffing, the recognition of revenue for items that had not really been sold to distributors.

On October 12, 2001, recently hired attorney Nancy Temple sent perhaps the most famous e-mail in business history, suggesting that a Houston partner remind the Enron engagement team of Andersen's documentation and retention policy. Auditors had been trained for decades that only final workpapers should be retained in audit files; preliminary schedules and draft memos should be destroyed.

The team proceeded to shred many documents even though an SEC investigation seemed likely in light of Enron's financial problems. The federal government subsequently indicted Andersen on one count of violating a law that forbids "corrupt persuasion" of others to withhold documents from official proceedings. A jury found Andersen guilty in June 2002. After an appellate court affirmation, the U.S. Supreme Court unanimously reversed the decision in 2005 and remarked how little culpability was required in the jury instructions to find Andersen guilty.

However, a criminal conviction represents a death sentence for an auditing firm. The blowups at Global Crossing and WorldCom erased any remaining confidence in Andersen. This professional services firm with 85,000 employees in 84 countries serving 100,000 clients closed its doors for business on August 31, 2002.

Andersen alumni constitute a who's who of accounting professionals. Arthur Wyatt, Edmund Jenkins, and G. Michael Crooch of the FASB; industry critic Leonard Spacek; AICPA research director Carman Blough; U.S. Comptroller General Charles Bowsher; theoretician Maurice Moonitz; and accounting lexicographer Eric Kohler all had worked for this proud firm.

The death of Andersen, together with the mergers of Ernst & Whinney with Arthur Young (1989), Deloitte Haskins & Sells with Touche Ross (1990), and Price Waterhouse with Coopers & Lybrand (1998), reduced the auditing industry's Big Eight to the Six Pack and then to the Final Four (with KPMG).

Three huge bankruptcies and loss of a major auditing firm stoked congressional fires. In late July lawmakers passed the Sarbanes-Oxley Act of 2002 (SOX), governance legislation "designed in a panic and rushed through in a blinding fervor of moral indignation."[26] The law reaffirmed that financial accountants and their auditors owe primary allegiance to innocent investors and lenders despite the awkward fact that these third parties do not directly compensate statement preparers and reviewers.

The Public Companies Accounting Oversight Board was established by SOX to register and monitor CPA firms. The law forbade auditors from engaging in many nonaudit services that would create a perceived conflict of interest. Section 302 required CEOs and CFOs to certify in writing that financial accounting numbers are correct. The rule attacked Jeffrey Skilling's excuse that he was not an accountant. Senior executives would now have to understand the debits and credits of significant accounting policies associated with SEC filings.

Section 404, the most onerous, required management and auditors to document internal control systems and evaluate their effectiveness. Auditors must report whether deficiencies identified constitute material weaknesses. A public corporation's annual report must then include the independent auditor's opinion on both financial statement accuracy and control system effectiveness.

Two University of Illinois accounting professors estimated that at the end of 2004, Section 404 internal controls documentation efforts consumed 130 million hours of time (worth perhaps $13 billion) without a shred of evidence that this effort would protect the investing public.[27]

Researchers had found a link between lax governance (e.g., chairman and CEO are the same person, non-CEO managers serve on employers' board, infrequent meetings) and a high level of accounting discretion (abnormal accruals, earnings smoothing, consistently favorable quarterly earnings surprises). However, they found no evidence that these issues led to consistently inferior security returns.[28] At the end of the day, good governance rests with the selection of a firm's CEO.

It's worth noting that SOX did create auditing jobs and may have resurrected interest in the CPA profession. Scandals allowed an auditor to become a potential hero, an Eliot Ness of financial reporting. From 2001 to 2004, the University of Illinois saw a 66 percent increase in undergraduate accounting majors and the University of Michigan saw a 76 percent increase in accounting master's students in the same period.[29]

There's no shame in losing money. American business history comes chock-full of failed business ideas. What is shameful is management action to conceal losses to dupe innocent investors and creditors. This is how FASB member Katherine Schipper defined accounting scandal.[30]

Too much debt undid Enron, Global Crossing, and World-Com. The telecom frenzy simply made it too easy for executives to borrow money to finance ill-conceived projects and acquisitions. Misleading financial reports drew in unsuspecting shareholders and lenders and magnified financial consequences of poor business decisions. Accounting errors indeed reversed as more information came to light, but a lot of people got hurt in the process.

15

EPILOGUE

No snowflake in an avalanche ever feels responsible.

—Voltaire

New York City mayor Ed Koch made famous the phrase "How am I doing?" U.S. accounting spawned four dialects to help corporations answer this question. Financial accounting offered outsiders information about the likelihood of debt repayment and future dividends. Tax accounting allowed the IRS to calculate its share of corporate income. Cost accounting helped management control operations. And statutory accounting let regulators monitor capital adequacy. These dialects developed in the absence of any unifying theory.

Financial accounting, the doyenne, emerged as a tangled collection of rules shaped by messy business practices. Even though reporting practices matter little over the long run, experience with the investment tax credit, troubled debt restructuring, oil and gas exploration, and stock options shows how politics hobbled the standard setting process. Government and business acceptance of diverse accounting treatment for income tax loss carryforwards and pro forma earnings demonstrated little concern for reporting the same transaction in varied ways. This discretion invited trouble.

Nevertheless financial accounting proved incredibly useful by reducing millions of transactions to a few numbers. No other tool matches financial reporting's ability to summarize. For this reason many people used accounting for contracting purposes, which created another problem. The Heisenberg uncertainty principle says that the more that is known about a subatomic particle's position, the less that can be known about its momentum. The act of observation disturbs the subject. The more importance users attach to accounting figures, the less comfort users can take in numbers' reliability.

Tying compensation, debt repayment, tax liabilities, or business licenses to accounting balances inevitably influences how managers report figures. Higher stakes simply put more pressure on statement preparers. Newswire and journalist discussions about making or missing quarterly numbers add fuel to the fire. The threat of earnings surprises distracts some CEOs from their job of building businesses. Some managers cave in to pressure to make their numbers each quarter.

With the rise of earnings aggregation services, certain CEOs insisted on reporting smooth earnings trajectories despite overwhelming evidence that markets eventually see through accounting tricks. The vast majority of financial accounting decisions have no consequence on cash flows and cumulative earnings. The train wreck of 2002 reinforced the point that successful business models do not rest on financial accounting principles. Good numbers don't compensate for bad management.

Wider acceptance of the efficient markets hypothesis (EMH), capital asset pricing model (CAPM), and Black-Scholes valuation model may have dampened accounting abuses during the telecom bubble. Research related to EMH suggested investors eventually see through gimmicks when setting security prices, CAPM efforts showed that investors do not necessarily punish raw earnings volatility, and acceptance of option pricing models may have led to expensing of grants and more intelligent use of this leveraged incentive tool.

However, academics haven't helped their own cause. Accounting remains a trade passed from master to apprentice. Complex, math-laden academic papers have shown little ability to influence financial statement preparers. Researchers should have devoted more time explaining key concepts to experienced practitioners. Sadly, this effort does not help aspiring professors obtain tenure.

Accounting scandal continued after the telecom bubble. Controversy enveloped Fannie Mae's and Freddie Mac's use of hedge accounting for derivatives positions, AIG's treatment of finite-risk reinsurance contracts, and Krispy Kreme's handling of related party transactions. It's not clear we have learned much from the events of 2002.

The federal government's first attempt to prosecute violation of Sarbanes-Oxley (SOX) Section 302 (certification of accounting numbers by CEOs and CFOs) ended in failure. Richard Scrushy, a onetime gas station attendant, earned a respiratory therapy diploma from the University of Alabama at Birmingham in 1974 and founded HealthSouth 10 years later.[1] The firm grew to become the nation's largest provider of outpatient surgery and rehabilitative health care services.

Its 2001 annual report boasted that the firm maintained the second-longest streak for meeting or exceeding analysts' earnings expectations. Things fell apart in mid-2002 when the government announced plans to revise Medicare reimbursement rules for certain treatments, which would reduce revenue. The share price dropped from $15.90 in the second quarter of 2002 to $0.08 in the first quarter of 2003. The New York Stock Exchange delisted the stock.

A swarm of auditors, consultants, and lawyers descended on the troubled firm. HealthSouth avoided bankruptcy and, in June 2005, filed a Form 10-K with 2002 and 2003 financial statements plus restated financials for 2000 and 2001. Among other things, HealthSouth disclosed the results shown in Table 15.1 (amounts in millions, except per share figures).

Table 15.1   HealthSouth Restatements for 2000 and 2001

	Year Ended December 31, 2000		Year Ended December 31, 2001	
	As Reported	Restated	As Reported	Restated
Revenues	$4,195	$3,498	$4,380	$3,553
Net income (loss)	278	(364)	202	(191)
Diluted EPS	0.71	**(0.94)**	0.51	**(0.49)**

The difference between balances as previously reported and as restated satisfies anyone's definition of materiality. The federal government charged that HealthSouth inflated cumulative income by $2.6 billion over the period 1996 through 2002.

Five former HealthSouth CFOs agreed to plead guilty to federal criminal charges in exchange for testimony against Scrushy. The Justice Department argued that such large accounting misstatements could not possibly have been pulled off without CEO involvement. Scrushy had signed off on HealthSouth's financial statements.

Yet, an Alabama jury acquitted Scrushy of all 36 counts against him. Scrushy's experience serves as an interesting counterpoint to that of WorldCom's Bernie Ebbers, who was convicted of accounting fraud. One analysis showed that Scrushy's prosecutors did not prove motive. Scrushy had not borrowed heavily against his stock, while Ebbers levered his WorldCom stock position through margin loans. Ebbers faced financial ruin from a modest drop in his company's share price and resulting margin calls, goes this argument, while Scrushy simply lost money.[2] The deterrent value of SOX Section 302 remains unclear.

These structural problems suggest that today's financial accounting issues will continue into the future. Resources spent to create a conceptual framework will likely show little benefit. Accounting will remain a pragmatic tool full of idiosyncrasies. A linguist might as well try to rewrite English to eliminate grammar and spelling exceptions.

Neither clearly articulated rules nor well-crafted principles will solve these problems, either. Experience with pooling of interests, leases, and loss contingencies suggests neither bright-line rules nor well-conceived principles guarantee fair financial reporting.

Accounting scandal, the deliberate concealment of accounting information to unfairly influence outsiders, ultimately represents a failure of statement preparers, not auditors, regulators, educators, standard setters, or legislators. Blame rests squarely on controllers and their bosses. No control system can ever guard completely against bad management behavior. The only workable solution is for corporations to select CEOs with impeccable integrity.

NOTES

CHAPTER 1   Double-Entry

1. Carr, *What Is History?*, Chapter 1.
2. Hudson, *History by Numbers*, p. 37.
3. Previts and Merino, *History of Accountancy*, p. 175.
4. Micklethwait and Woolridge, *Company*, p. 128.
5. Hendriksen, *Accounting Theory*, p. 59.
6. Flegm, *Accounting*, p. 31.
7. Berle and Means, *Modern Corporation*, pp. 10–11, 47.

CHAPTER 2   Railroads

1. Ambrose, *Nothing Like It*, p. 57.
2. Ibid., p. 377.
3. Baskin and Miranti, *History of Corporate Finance*, p. 136.
4. Previts and Merino, pp. 69, 110.
5. Hawkins, "Development of Modern," pp. 135–136.
6. Ibid., p. 143.
7. Skeel, *Icarus in the Boardroom*, p. 57.
8. Hendriksen, pp. 38–39.
9 Sylla, "Historical Primer."
10. Ibid.

11. Baskin and Miranti, p. 148.

12. Carey, *Rise of the Accounting Profession*, vol. 1, p. 26.

13. Hendriksen, p. 23.

14. Lowenstein, *Origins of the Crash*, p. 164.

15. Stickney and Weil, *Financial Accounting*, p. 793.

16. Ripley, *Main Street and Wall Street*, p. 174.

17. Carey, vol. 1, p. 68.

18. Hendriksen, p. 41.

19. Sivakumar and Waymire, "Enforceable Accounting Rules."

20. Hendriksen, p. 42.

21. Previts and Merino, p. 224.

22. Carey, vol. 1, p. 29.

CHAPTER 3   Taxes

1. Joseph, *Origins of the American Income Tax*, p. 33.

2. Ibid., pp. 89–92.

3. Scholes et al., *Taxes and Business Strategy*, pp. 30–31.

4. Federer, *Interesting History of Income Tax*, p. 13.

5. Rossotti, *Many Unhappy Returns*, p. 79.

6. Ibid., pp. 14, 202.

7. Scholes et al., p. 23.

8. McAnly, "How LIFO Began."

9. Cooper, Malone, and McFadden-Wade, "Establishing the LIFO Conformity Rule."

10. Hendriksen, p. 345.

11. Paton, "Comments on 'A Statement of Accounting Principles.' "

12. Sunder, "Stock Price and Risk Related to Accounting Changes."

13. Biddle, "Paying FIFO Taxes."

14. *Accounting Trends & Techniques*, p. 177.

15. Hendriksen, p. 119.

CHAPTER 4   Costs

1. Rossotti, p. 111.

2. Johnson and Kaplan, *Relevance Lost*, p. 21.

3. Previts and Merino, p. 58.

4. Chandler, *Scale and Scope*, pp. 54–55.

5. Johnson and Kaplan, p. 112.
6. Garsten, " 'Whiz Kids' Reinvent Automaker."
7. Kreisler, "Robert McNamara Interview."
8. Kieso, Weygandt, and Warfield, *Intermediate Accounting*, p. 404.
9. Carey, vol. 1, p. 142.
10. Johnson and Kaplan, p. 139.
11. Flegm, p. 16.
12. Carey, vol. 1, pp. 311–312.
13. Clark, *Studies in the Economics of Overhead Costs.*
14. McKinsey, *Managerial Accounting*, p. xii.
15 in business analysis: H. Thomas Johnson, pp. 154-157.
16. Vatter, *Managerial Accounting.*
17. Dean, "Measuring the Productivity of Capital."
18. Cooper and Bingham, "Mayers Tap, Inc."
19. Toffler, *Final Accounting*, pp. 101–108.
20. Kaplan and Norton, "Balanced Scorecard."

CHAPTER 5   Disclosure

1. Baskin and Miranti, p. 190.
2. Berle and Means, p. 60.
3. Ibid., p. 297.
4. Baskin and Miranti, p. 232.
5. Ripley, p. 187.
6. Hoxsey, "Accounting for Investors."
7. Berle and Means, p. 211.
8. Galbraith, *Great Crash 1929.*
9. Benston, "Required Disclosure."
10. Barton and Waymire, "Investor Protection."
11. Benston, "Require Disclosure."
12. Wharton seminar, "Pension Fund and Investment Management," Philadelphia, Pennsylvania, June 2000.
13. Example inspired by Jeffrey Jaffe at June 2000 Wharton seminar.
14. Yee, "Interim Reporting Frequency."
15. Flesher, Miranti, and Previts, "First Century of the CPA."
16. Carey, vol. 1, pp. 184–188.
17. Carey, vol. 2, p. 23.
18. "Stern Stewart Roundtable," comment by Jerold Zimmerman, p. 7.

19. Chambers, "Fair Financial Reporting."
20. Financial Management Network, "Accountable Accounting."
21. Bruner, *Deals from Hell*, pp. 106–107.

CHAPTER 6   Standards

1. Gullapalli, "Excise Taxes Muddy Comparisons."
2. Briloff and Anthony, "By Whom and How Should."
3. Baxter, "Accounting Standards."
4. D'Arcy, "Insurance Price Deregulation."
5. Committee on Accounting Procedure, paragraph 4.
6. Hendriksen, p. 71.
7. Moonitz, "Obtaining Agreement," p. 15.
8. Spacek, *Growth of Arthur Andersen*, p. 9.
9. Ibid., p. 43.
10. Ibid., p. 173.
11. Ibid., p. 238.
12. Ibid., pp. 60–62.
13. Ibid., p. 248.
14. Previts and Merino, pp. 310–311.
15. Zeff, "Work of the Special Committee."
16. Flegm, p. 83.
17. Zeff, "Special Committee."
18. Ibid.
19. Ibid.
20. Hawkins, "Financial Accounting."
21. *BusinessWeek*, "Matter of Principle," p. 55.
22. *Senate Reporter*, November 1, 1971. 92–347, at 45.
23. Flegm, p. 97.
24. Moonitz, p. 23.
25. Evans, *Accounting Theory*, p. 86.
26. Ibid., p. 102.
27. Staubus, "Cherry Pickers' Friend."
28. Kieso, Weygandt, and Warfield, pp. 747–748.
29. Sunder, "Properties of Accounting Numbers."
30. Ibid.
31. Kieso, Weygandt, and Warfield, p. 567.
32. Evans, p. 188.

33. Baxter.
34. Flegm, p. 57.
35. Leuz, "IAS versus US GAAP."

CHAPTER 7   Science

1. Briloff, "By Whom and How Should."
2. Hawkins, "Development of Modern Financial Reporting."
3. Previts and Merino, p. 151.
4. Copeland, *And Mark an Era,* p. 22.
5. Zeff, *American Accounting Association,* pp. 4–5.
6. Ibid., p. 5.
7. Ibid., pp. 43–45.
8. Moonitz, p. 12.
9. Zeff, *American Accounting Association,* p. 49.
10. Flegm, p. 40.
11. Copeland, p. 158.
12. Nelson, "What's New about Accounting Education Change."
13. Sorter, "Beyond Emptiness and Blindness."
14. Fama, "Efficient Capital Markets."
15. Jensen, "Performance of Mutual Funds."
16. Watts and Zimmerman, *Positive Accounting Theory,* p. 86.
17. Ball and Brown, "Empirical Evaluation."
18. Watts and Zimmerman, p. 57.
19. Sorter.
20. Watts, "Evolution of Economics-Based Empirical Research."
21. Burton, "Fair Presentation."
22. Flegm, p. 178.
23. Wyatt, "Efficient Market Theory."
24. Amershi and Sunder, "Failure of Stock Prices."
25. Wolk, Dodd, and Tearney, *Accounting Theory,* p. 211.

CHAPTER 8   Inflation

1. Author's correspondence with Mark Sniderman, director of research, Federal Reserve Bank of Cleveland.
2. Mednick, "Accounting and Financial Reporting."
3. Burton, "Fair Presentation."

4. Mednick.
5. Watts and Zimmerman, p. 174.
6. FASB, Statement 33, paragraphs 12 and 14.
7. Davidson, "Inflation That Won't Go Away."
8. St. Goar, "Experiment Abandoned."
9. FASB, Statement 89, paragraph 4.
10. *Accounting Trends & Techniques*, p. 147.
11. Flegm, p. 200.

CHAPTER 9   Volatility

1. Burton, "Revisiting the Capital Asset Pricing Model."
2. Pratt, *Cost of Capital*, p. 3.
3. Ryan et al., "Recommendations on Hedge Accounting."
4. Forbes, "Why Can't Accountants Be Practical?"
5. Wolk, Dodd, and Tearney, p. 653.
6. Ibid., p. 653.
7. Ibid., p. 536.
8. Tietjen.
9. Benston et al., *Following the Money*, p. 47.
10. Wolk, Dodd, and Tearney, p. 545.
11. Cited by Wolk, Dodd, and Tearney, p. 546.
12. Skeel, p. 63.
13. "Market Value: The Debate Rages."

CHAPTER 10   Intangibles

1. "Stern Stewart Roundtable," comment by Joel Stern, p. 23.
2. Ghemawat, *Strategy and the Business Landscape*, p. 44.
3. CAP, Bulletin 24, paragraph 1.
4. FASB, Statement 2, paragraph 12.
5. Briloff and Anthony, "By Whom and How Should."
6. Flegm, p. 103.
7. Lowenstein, p. 73.
8. Bruner, p. 273.
9. Hirst and Hopkins, *Earnings: Measurement, Disclosure*, p. 6.
10. Cohen, "Issues and Outlook 2005," p. 10.
11. Hawkins, *Financial Reporting Practices*, pp. 298–300.
12. Briloff, "Dirty Pooling."

13. Fioriti and Brady, "Anatomy of a Pooling."
14. Barnes and Servaes, "Stock Market Response to Changes."
15. Weber, "Shareholder Wealth Effects."

CHAPTER 11 Debt

1. Skeel, pp. 119–121.
2. Bruck, *Predators' Ball*, pp. 261–262.
3. Monson, "Conceptual Framework."
4. Abdel-Khalik, *Economic Effects on Lessees.*
5. Weil, "How Leases Play a Shadowy Role in Accounting."
6. Leary, "Factors Influencing the Level of Environmental Liability Disclosure."
7. *Accounting Trends & Techniques*, p. 76.
8. Foust and Byrnes, "Gone Flat."

CHAPTER 12 Options

1. Berle and Means, pp. 180–183.
2. Dean, "Employee Stock Options."
3. Hendriksen, p. 532.
4. Arthur Andersen & Co., *Accounting and Reporting Problems*, p. 59.
5. APB, Opinion 25, paragraph 20.
6. Black and Scholes, "Pricing of Options and Corporate Liabilities."
7. Fox, "Next Best Thing."
8. Ibid.
9. Skeel, p. 152.
10. Lowenstein, p. 44.
11. FASB, Statement 123, paragraph 376.
12. Schneider, "Who Rules Accounting?"
13. Silva and Finnegan, "Analytical Implications."
14. Aboody and Kasznik, "CEO Stock Option Awards."
15. Fox, "Next Best Thing."
16. Garg and Wilson, "Expensing of Options."

CHAPTER 13 Earnings

1. Degeorge, Patel, and Zeckhauser, "Earnings Management" and Hirst, pp. 45–56.
2. Hirst and Hopkins, pp. 34–35.

3. CAP, Bulletin 32, paragraph 2.

4. Hendriksen, p. 551.

5. Ameen, "Six Sigma Accounting."

6. Tietjen, "Financial Reporting Responsibilities."

7. Berenson, *The Number*, p. 92.

8. "I/B/E/S for Academic Users."

9. Fox, "Learn to Play the Earnings Game."

10. Hirst and Hopkins, p. 47.

11. Lowenstein, p. 29.

12. Johnson and Kaplan, pp. 204–205.

13. Watts and Zimmerman, pp. 146–148, 201.

14. Flegm, p. 226.

15. Welch, *Jack: Straight from the Gut*, p. 225.

16. Cheng and Warfield, "Equity Incentives and Earnings Management."

17. Burgstahler and Dichev, "Earnings Management to Avoid Earnings Decreases."

18. Bartov, Givoly, and Hayn "Rewards to Meeting or Beating."

19. Graham, Harvey, and Rajgopal, "Economic Implications."

20. Lowenstein, pp. 66–67.

21. Levitt, " 'Numbers Game.' "

22. Morgenson, "Pennies That Aren't from Heaven."

23. Wallison, "Give Us Disclosure, Not Audits."

24. Johnson and Schwartz, "Everyday Pricing."

25. Ibid.

26. Francis et al., "Costs of Capital."

27. Kieso, Weygandt, and Warfield, p. 1156.

CHAPTER 14   SOX

1. "Largest Bankruptcies, 1980 to Present."

2. Baxter.

3. Ameen.

4. Turner, "State of Financial Reporting Today."

5. Benston, "Quality of Corporate Financial Statements."

6. Brewster, *Unaccountable*, p. 229.

7. Holtzman, Venuti, and Fonfeder, "Enron and the Raptors."

8. Squires et al., *Inside Arthur Andersen*, p. 9.

9. Bruck, pp. 51, 259.

10. Arthur Andersen & Co., pp. 79–83.
11. Tauzin, "Capacity Swaps by Global Crossing and Qwest."
12. Brown, "Global Crossing Scores a Bankruptcy Bonanza."
13. Pulliam and Latour, "Trial of WorldCom's Ebbers."
14. Ibid.
15. Blumenstein and Grant, "Former Chief Tries to Redeem the Calls."
16. Latour and Young, "WorldCom's Sullivan Says He Told CEO."
17. Sorkin, "Ex-Chief and Aide Guilty of Looting Millions."
18. Frieswick, "How Audits Must Change."
19. *Economist*, "Credit-Rating Agencies."
20. Spacek, p. 183.
21. Squires et al., p. 76.
22. Previts and Merino, p. 400.
23. Squires et al., pp. 84–86.
24. Toffler, p. 130.
25. Ibid., p. 248.
26. *Economist*, "Damaged Goods."
27. Salomon and Peecher, "SOX 404—A Billion Here, a Billion There . . ."
28. Bowen, Rajgopal, and Venkatchalam, "Accounting Discretion."
29. Gullapalli, "Crunch This! CPAs Become the New BMOCs."
30. Financial Management Network.

CHAPTER 15   Epilogue

1. Morse and Terhune, "HealthSouth's Scrushy Is Acquitted."
2. Terhune, Morse, and Latour, "Why Scrushy Won, Ebbers Lost."

BIBLIOGRAPHY

Most biographical information came from Ohio State University's Accounting Hall of Fame, available at http://fisher.osu.edu/acctmis/hall/. Most speeches cited came from Baruch College's Saxe lecture series, available at http://newman.baruch.cuny.edu/digital/saxe/toc.htm.

Abdel-Khalik, A. Rashad. *The Economic Effects on Lessees of FASB Statement No. 13, Accounting for Leases.* Stamford, CT: Financial Accounting Standards Board, 1981.

Abdel-Khalik, A. Rashad. "Managers' Emphasis on the Short Run: Contrast with the Japanese and Implications for Accounting." Speech at Baruch College, December 14, 1982. http://newman.baruch.cuny.edu/digital/saxe/saxe_1982/abdel_khalik_82.htm.

Aboody, David, and Ron Kasznik. "CEO Stock Option Awards and Corporate Voluntary Disclosures." May 22, 2000. http://ssrn.com/abstract=144589.

Accounting Trends & Techniques 2004. 58th ed. New York: American Institute of Certified Public Accountants.

Ambrose, Stephen E. *Nothing Like It in the World: The Men Who Built the Transcontinental Railroad 1863–1869.* New York: Simon & Schuster, 2000.

Ameen, Philip D. "Six Sigma Accounting in the New Millennium." Speech at Baruch College, November 1, 1999. http://newman .baruch.cuny.edu/digital/saxe/saxe_1999/amen_1999.htm.

Amershi, Amin, and Shyam Sunder. "Failure of Stock Prices to Discipline Managers in a Rational Expectations Economy." *Journal of Accounting Research* (Autumn 1987).

Arthur Andersen & Co. *Accounting and Reporting Problems of the Accounting Profession.* September 1960.

Ascarelli, Silvia. "Citing Sarbanes, Foreign Companies Flee US Exchanges." *Wall Street Journal,* September 20, 2004.

Ball, Ray, and Philip Brown. "An Empirical Evaluation of Accounting Income Numbers." *Journal of Accounting Research* (Autumn 1968).

Bandler, James, and John Hechinger. "Six Figures in Xerox Case Are Fined $22 Million." *Wall Street Journal,* June 6, 2003.

Barnes, Ronnie, and Henri Servaes. "The Stock Market Response to Changes in Business Combinations Accounting." London Business School working paper, February 28, 2002.

Barton, Jan, and Gregory Waymire. "Investor Protection under Unregulated Financial Reporting." Emory University working paper, September 15, 2003.

Bartov, Eli, Dan Givoly, and Carla Hayn. "The Rewards to Meeting or Beating Earnings Expectations." *Journal of Accounting & Economics* 33 (2002): 173–204.

Baskin, Jonathan B., and Paul J. Miranti Jr. *A History of Corporate Finance.* Cambridge, UK: Cambridge University Press, 1997.

Baxter, William T. "Accounting Standards: Boon or Curse." Speech at Baruch College, February 13, 1979. http://newman.baruch .cuny.edu/digital/saxe/saxe_1978/baxter_79.htm.

Beaver, William H. *Financial Reporting: An Accounting Revolution.* Upper Saddle River, NJ: Prentice Hall, 1998.

Benston, George J. "The Quality of Corporate Financial Statements and Their Auditors before and after Enron." *Policy Analysis,* November 6, 2003. Washington, DC: Cato Project on Corporate Governance, Audit and Tax Reform, 2003.

Benston, George J. "Required Disclosure and the Stock Market: An Evaluation of the Securities Exchange Act of 1934." *American Economic Review* (March 1973).

Benston, George J. "The Role and Limitations of Financial Accounting and Auditing for Financial Market Discipline." November 20, 2003, draft working paper.

Benston, George J., Michael Bromwich, Robert E. Litan, and Alfred Wagenhofer. *Following the Money: The Enron Failure and the State of Corporate Disclosure.* Washington, DC: Brookings Institution Press, 2003.

Berenson, Alex. *The Number.* New York: Random House, 2003.

Berle, Adolf A., Jr., and Gardiner C. Means. *The Modern Corporation and Private Property.* New York: Macmillan, 1933.

Biddle, Gary. "Paying FIFO Taxes: Your Favorite Charity?" *Wall Street Journal,* January 19, 1981.

Black, Fischer, and Myron Scholes. "The Pricing of Options and Corporate Liabilities." *Journal of Political Economy* (May–June 1973).

Blough, Carman G. *Practical Applications of Accounting Standards.* New York: American Institute of Certified Public Accountants, 1957.

Blumenstein, Rebecca, and Peter Grant. "Former Chief Tries to Redeem the Calls He Made at AT&T." *Wall Street Journal,* May 26, 2004.

Boulton, E. S., Barry D. Libert, and Steve M. Samek. *Cracking the Value Code: How Successful Businesses Are Creating Wealth in the New Economy.* New York: HarperCollins, 2000.

Bowen, Robert M., Shivaram Rajgopal, and Mohan Venkatchalam, "Accounting Discretion, Corporate Governance and Firm Performance," March 2004. http://ssrn.com/abstract=367940.

Brandeis, Louis D., and Melvin I. Urofsky (Editor). *Other People's Money and How the Bankers Use It.* New York: Bedford/St. Martin's, 1995.

Brewster, Mike. *Unaccountable: How the Accounting Profession Forfeited a Public Trust.* Hoboken, NJ: John Wiley & Sons, 2003.

Briloff, Abraham J. "Dirty Pooling." *Accounting Review* (July 1967).

Briloff, Abraham J., and Robert N. Anthony. "By Whom and How Should Accounting Standards Be Determined and Implemented?" Debate at Baruch College, February 27, 1978. http://newman.baruch.cuny.edu/digital/saxe/saxe_1977/briloff_78.htm.

Brown, Ken. "Global Crossing Scores a Bankruptcy Bonanza." *Wall Street Journal,* March 11, 2004.

Bruck, Connie. *The Predators' Ball: The Inside Story of Drexel Burnham and the Rise of the Junk Bond Raiders.* New York: Penguin Books, 1989.

Bruner, Robert F. *Deals from Hell.* Hoboken, NJ: John Wiley & Sons, 2005.

Burgstahler, David, and Ilia Dichev. "Earnings Management to Avoid Earnings Decreases and Losses." *Journal of Accounting and Economics,* 24 (1997): 99–126.

Burton, John C. "Fair Presentation: Another View." Speech given at Baruch College, February 18, 1975. http://newman.baruch .cuny.edu/digital/saxe/saxe_1974/burton_75.htm.

Burton, Jonathon. "Revisiting the Capital Asset Pricing Model." *Dow Jones Asset Manager,* May/June 1998.

BusinessWeek. "A Matter of Principle Splits CPAs." *BusinessWeek,* January 26, 1963.

Carey, John L. *The Rise of the Accounting Profession.* Vols. 1 and 2. New York: American Institute of Certified Public Accountants, 1969.

Carr, E. H. *What Is History?* Hampshire, UK: Palgrave, 2001.

Chambers, Raymond J. "Fair Financial Reporting in Law and Practice." Speech at Baruch College, October 28, 1976. http://newman .baruch.cuny.edu/digital/saxe/saxe_1976/chambers_76.htm.

Chandler, Alfred D., Jr. *Scale and Scope: The Dynamics of Industrial Capitalism.* Cambridge, MA: Harvard University Press, 1990.

Cheng, Qiang, and Terry D. Warfield. "Equity Incentives and Earnings Management." June 2004. http://ssrn.com/abstract=457840.

Clark, J. Maurice. *Studies in the Economics of Overhead Costs.* Chicago, IL: University of Chicago Press, 1923.

Cohen, Abby Joseph. "Issues and Outlook 2005." New York: Goldman Sachs, March 2005.

Committee on Accounting Procedure. "Restatement and Revision of Accounting Research Bulletin." New York: American Institute of Certified Public Accountants, 1953.

The Complete Internal Revenue Code. New York: Research Institute of America, 2003.

Cooper, Robin, and Glenn Bingham. "Mayers Tap, Inc." Harvard Business School Case 9-185-024, -025, and -026. Boston: Harvard Business School Publishing, 1984.

Cooper, William D., Charles F. Malone, and Gwendolyn McFadden-Wade. "Establishing the LIFO Conformity Rule." www.nsysscpa.org/cpa journal/1996/0796/newsviews/nv7.htm.

Copeland, Melvin T. *And Mark an Era: The Story of the Harvard Business School.* Boston: Little, Brown, 1958.

D'Arcy, Stephen D. "Insurance Price Deregulation: The Illinois Experience." May 14, 2001. www.business.uiuc.edu/~s-darcy/Fin 431/2005/readings/Illinois%20Experience%20(Revised%202).doc.

Davidson, Sidney. "The Inflation That Won't Go Away and How to Account for It." Speech at Baruch College, November 5, 1979. http://newman.baruch.cuny.edu/digital/saxe/saxe_1979/davidson_79.htm.

Dean, Arthur H. "Employee Stock Options." 66 *Harvard Law Review* 1403, June 1953.

Dean, Joel. "Measuring the Productivity of Capital." *Harvard Business Review* (January–February 1954).

Degeorge, Francois, Jayendu Patel, and Richard Zeckhauser. "Earnings Management to Exceed Thresholds." *Journal of Business* 72, no. 1 (1999).

Economic History Services. www.eh.net/hmit/gdp/.

Economist. "Credit-Rating Agencies: Three Is No Crowd." *Economist,* March 26, 2005.

Economist. "Damaged Goods: The American Economic Model Is Doing All Right. It Could Be Doing Even Better." *Economist,* May 19, 2005.

Evans, Thomas. *Accounting Theory: Contemporary Accounting Issues.* Mason, OH: Thomson South-Western, 2003.

Fama, Eugene F. "Efficient Capital Markets: A Review of Theory and Empirical Work." *Journal of Finance* (May 1970).

Federal Reserve Board. "Uniform Accounts." *Federal Reserve Bulletin,* April 1917.

Federer, William J. *The Interesting History of Income Tax.* St. Louis, MO: Amerisearch, 2004.

Financial Management Network. "Accountable Accounting: Principles or Rules?" Videotaped roundtable discussion hosted by Baruch College's Robert Zicklin Center for Corporate Integrity. Hawthorne, NY: Smart Pros, December 2004 and January 2005.

Fioriti, Andrew A., and Thomas J. Brady. "Anatomy of a Pooling: The AT&T/NCR Merger." *Ohio CPA Journal* (October 1994).

Flegm, Eugene H. *Accounting: How to Meet the Challenges of Relevance and Regulation.* New York: John Wiley & Sons, 1984.

Flesher, Dale L., Paul J. Miranti, and Gary John Previts. "The First Century of the CPA." *Journal of Accountancy* (October 1996).

Forbes, Malcolm S., Jr. "Why Can't Accountants Be Practical?" *Forbes,* June 12, 1978.

Foust, Dean, and Nanette Byrnes. "Gone Flat." *BusinessWeek*, December 20, 2004.

Fox, Justin. "Learn to Play the Earnings Game." *Fortune*, March 31, 1997.

Fox, Justin. "The Next Best Thing to Free Money." *Fortune*, July 7, 1997.

Fox, Justin. "A Startling Notion—The Whole Truth." *Fortune*, November 24, 1997.

Francis, Jennifer, Ryan Z. LaFond, Per Olsson, and Katherine Schipper. "Costs of Capital and Earnings Attributes." May 2003. http://ssrn.com/abstract=414125.

Frankfurter, George M., Bob G. Wood, and James Wansley. *Dividend Policy Theory and Practice*. San Diego, CA: Elsevier Press, 2003.

Frieswick, Kris. "How Audits Must Change: Auditors Face More Pressure to Find Fraud." *CFO*, July 2003.

Galbraith, John Kenneth. *The Great Crash 1929*. New York: Time Inc. 1962.

Garg, Ashish, and William Wilson. "Expensing of Options: What Do the Markets Say?" Ernst & Young's *CrossCurrents*, Fall 2003.

Garsten, Ed. " 'Whiz Kids' Reinvent Automaker." *Detroit News*, June 9, 2003.

Ghemawat, Pankaj. *Strategy and the Business Landscape*. Upper Saddle River, NJ: Pearson Prentice Hall, 2006.

Goff, John, "Who's the Boss?" *CFO*, September 2004.

Graham, John Robert, Campbell R. Harvey, and Shivaram Rajgopal. "The Economic Implications of Corporate Financial Reporting." September 13, 2004. ssrn.com/abstract=491627.

Greene, Richard. "The Joys of Leasing." *Forbes*, November 24, 1980.

Gullapalli, Diya. "Crunch This! CPAs Become the New BMOCs." *Wall Street Journal*, July 29, 2004.

Gullapalli, Diya. "Excise Taxes Muddy Comparisons." *Wall Street Journal*, July 23, 2004.

Hawkins, David F. "The Development of Modern Financial Reporting Practices among American Manufacturing Corporations." *Business History Review* (Autumn 1963).

Hawkins, David F. "Financial Accounting, the Standards Board and Economic Development." Speech at Baruch College, November 12, 1973. http://newman.baruch.cuny.edu/digital/saxe/saxe_1973/Hawkins _73.htm.

Hawkins, David F. *Financial Reporting Practices of Corporations.* Homewood, IL: Dow Jones–Irwin, 1972.

Hendriksen, Eldon. *Accounting Theory.* Homewood, IL: Richard D. Irwin, 1970.

Hirst, D. Eric, and Patrick E. Hopkins. *Earnings: Measurement, Disclosure, and the Impact on Equity Valuation.* Charlottesville, VA: Association for Investment Management and Research, 2000.

Holtzman, Mark P., Elizabeth Venuti, and Robert Fonfeder. "Enron and the Raptors." *CPA Journal,* April 2003. www.nysscpa.org/cap journal/2003/0403/features/f042403.htm.

Hoxsey, J. M. B. "Accounting for Investors." *Journal of Accountancy* (October 1930).

Hudson, Pat. *History by Numbers.* New York: Oxford University Press, 2000.

"I/B/E/S for Academic Users." http://fisher.osu/fin/resources_data/ provider/ibes.htm.

Jenkins, Nicole, and Morton Pincus. "LIFO versus FIFO: Updating What We Have Learned." University of Iowa working paper, September 1998.

Jensen, Michael C. "The Performance of Mutual Funds in the Period 1945–1964." *Journal of Finance* (May 1968).

Jensen, Michael C., and William H. Meckling. "Theory of the Firm: Managerial Behavior, Agency Costs and Ownership Structure." *Journal of Financial Economics* (October 1976).

Johnson, H. Thomas, and Robert S. Kaplan. *Relevance Lost: The Rise and Fall of Management Accounting.* Boston: Harvard Business School Press, 1991.

Johnson, W. Bruce, and William C. Schwartz Jr. "Everyday Pricing: Do Pro Forma Earnings Mislead Investors?" *Investor Relations Quarterly* 5, no. 4.

Joseph, Richard J. *The Origins of the American Income Tax: The Revenue Act of 1894 and Its Aftermath.* Syracuse, NY: Syracuse University Press, 2004.

Kaplan, Robert S., and David P. Norton. "The Balanced Scorecard— Measures That Drive Performance." *Harvard Business Review* (January–February 1992).

Kieso, Donald E., Jerry J. Weygandt, and Terry D. Warfield. *Intermediate Accounting.* 10th ed. New York: John Wiley & Sons, 2001.

Kreisler, Harry. "Robert McNamara Interview: Conversations with History." Interview with Robert McNamara, Institute of International Studies, University of California, Berkeley, April 16, 1996. http://globetrotter.berkeley.edu/McNamara/mcnamara1.html.

"The Largest Bankruptcies, 1980 to Present." www.bankruptcydata .com/Research/15_largest.htm.

Latour, Almar, and Shawn Young. "WorldCom's Sullivan Says He Told CEO of Problems." *Wall Street Journal,* February 9, 2005.

Leary, Carol. "Factors Influencing the Level of Environmental Liability Disclosure in 10-K Reports." Undated, unpublished paper. George Mason University.

Leuz, Christian. "IAS versus US GAAP: A 'New Market' Based Comparison." Wharton working paper, October 2000.

Levitt, Arthur. "The 'Numbers Game.' " Speech delivered at the NYU Center for Law and Business, September 28, 1998. www.sec.gov/ news/speech/speecharchive/1998/spch220.txt.

Levitt, Steven D., and Stephen J. Dubner. *Freakonomics: A Rogue Economist Explores the Hidden Side of Everything.* New York: William Morrow, 2005.

Lowenstein, Roger. *Origins of the Crash: The Great Bubble and Its Undoing.* New York: Penguin Press, 2004.

"Market Value: The Debate Rages." *Financial Executive,* January 1993.

Markowitz, Harry. "Portfolio Selection." *Journal of Finance* 7, no. 1 (March 1952): 77–91.

McAnly, Herbert. "How LIFO Began." *Management Accounting,* May 1975.

McKinsey, James O. *Managerial Accounting.* Chicago: University of Chicago Press, 1924.

Mednick, Robert. "Accounting and Financial Reporting in a High Inflation Environment." Paper presented to the Fourth Jerusalem Conference on Accountancy, November 1986.

Micklethwait, John, and Adrian Wooldridge. *The Company.* New York: Modern Library, 2003.

Monson, Dennis W. "The Conceptual Framework and Accounting for Leases." *Accounting Horizons,* September 2001.

Moonitz, Maurice. *Obtaining Agreement on Standards in the Accounting Profession.* Sarasota, FL: American Accounting Association, 1974.

Morgenson, Gretchen C. "Pennies That Aren't from Heaven." *New York Times,* November 7, 2004.

Morse, Dan, and Chad Terhune. "HealthSouth's Scrushy Is Acquitted." *Wall Street Journal,* June 29, 2005.

Nelson, Irvin T. "What's New about Accounting Education Change? An Historical Perspective on the Change Movement." *Accounting Horizons,* Fall 1995.

Ohio State University. *The Accounting Hall of Fame.* http://fisher.osu .edu/acctmis/hall/.

Paton, William A. "Comments on 'A Statement of Accounting Principles.' " *Journal of Accountancy* (March 1938).

Paton, William A., and A. C. Littleton. *An Introduction to Corporate Accounting Standards.* Sarasota, FL: American Accounting Association, 1940.

Pratt, Shannon P. *Cost of Capital: Estimation and Applications.* New York: John Wiley & Sons, 1998.

Previts, Gary John, and Barbara Dubis Merino. *A History of Accountancy in the United States: The Cultural Significance of Accounting.* Columbus, OH: Ohio State University Press, 1998.

Pulliam, Susan, and Almar Latour. "Trial of WorldCom's Ebbers Will Focus on Uneasy Partnership." *Wall Street Journal,* January 12, 2005.

Revsine, Lawrence, Daniel W. Collins, and W. Bruce Johnson. *Financial Reporting and Analysis.* 3rd ed. Upper Saddle River, NJ: Prentice Hall, 2005.

Ripley, William Z. *Main Street and Wall Street.* Boston: Little, Brown, 1927.

Rossotti, Charles O. *Many Unhappy Returns: One Man's Quest to Turn Around the Most Unpopular Organization in America.* Boston: Harvard Business School Press, 2005.

Ryan, Stephen G., et al. "Recommendations on Hedge Accounting and Accounting for Transfer of Financial Instruments." *Accounting Horizons,* March 2002.

Salomon, Ira, and Mark E. Peecher. "SOX 404—A Billion Here, a Billion There . . ." *Wall Street Journal,* November 9, 2004.

Schneider, Craig. "Who Rules Accounting?" *CFO,* August 2003.

Scholes, Myron S., Mark A. Wolfson, Merle Erickson, Edward L. Maydew, and Terry Shevlin. *Taxes and Business Strategy: A Planning Approach,* 2nd ed. Upper Saddle River, NJ: Prentice Hall, 2002.

Sharpe, William F. "Capital Asset Prices: A Theory of Market Equilibrium under Conditions of Risk." *Journal of Finance* (September 1964).

Silva, Dagmar, and Patrick Finnegan. "Analytical Implications of Employee Stock-Based Compensation." Moody's Investors Service, *Rating Methodology*, December 2002.

Sivakumar, Kumar N., and Gregory B. Waymire. "Enforceable Accounting Rules and Income Measurement by Early 20th Century Railroads." April 16, 2002. http://ssrn.com/abstract=308602.

Skeel, David. *Icarus in the Boardroom: The Fundamental Flaws in Corporate America and Where They Came From.* New York: Oxford University Press, 2005.

Sorkin, Andrew Ross. "Ex-Chief and Aide Guilty of Looting Millions at Tyco." *New York Times,* June 18, 2005.

Sorter, George. "Beyond Emptiness and Blindness: Is There a Hope for Accounting Research?" Speech at Baruch College, March 27, 1979. http://newman.baruch.cuny.edu/digital/saxe/saxe_1978/sorter_79.htm.

Spacek, Leonard. *The Growth of Arthur Andersen & Co. 1928–1973: An Oral History.* New York: Garland Publishing, 1989.

Squires, Susan E., Cynthia J. Smith, Lorna McDougall and William R. Yeack. *Inside Arthur Andersen: Shifting Values, Unexpected Consequences.* Upper Saddle River, NJ: FT Prentice Hall, 2003.

St. Goar, Jinny. "Experiment Abandoned." *Forbes,* November 18, 1985.

Staubus, George. "Cherry Pickers' Friend—FASB Proposal Caters to Banks, Insurers." *Barron's,* December 7, 1992.

"Stern Stewart Roundtable on Relationship Investing and Shareholder Communications," *Journal of Applied Corporate Finance* (Summer 1993).

Stewart, G. Bennett, III. "How to Fix Accounting—Measure and Report Economic Profit." *Journal of Applied Corporate Finance* (Spring 2003).

Stickney, Clyde, and Roman Weil. *Financial Accounting: An Introduction to Concepts, Methods and Uses.* 10th ed. Mason, OH: Thomson South-Western, 2003.

Sunder, Shyam. "Properties of Accounting Numbers under Full Costing and Successful-Efforts Costing in the Petroleum Industry." *Accounting Review* (January 1976).

Sunder, Shyam. "Stock Price and Risk Related to Accounting Changes in Inventory Valuation." *Accounting Review* (April 1975).

Sylla, Richard. "A Historical Primer on the Business of Credit Ratings." Paper prepared for conference on "The Role of Credit Reporting Systems in the International Economy," World Bank, Washington, DC, March 1–2, 2001.

Tauzin, W. J. "Billy." "Capacity Swaps by Global Crossing and Qwest: Sham Transactions Designed to Boost Revenues?" Witness List and Prepared Testimony, Subcommittee on Oversight and Investigations, Committee on Energy and Commerce, September 24, 2002. http://energycommerce.house.gov/107/Hearings/09242002 hearing725.

Terhune, Chad, Dan Morse, and Almar Latour. "Why Scrushy Won, Ebbers Lost." *Wall Street Journal,* June 30, 2005.

Tietjen, A. Carl. "Financial Reporting Responsibilities." Speech at Baruch College on April 7, 1975. http://newman.baruch.cuny .edu/digital/saxe/saxe_1974/tietjen_75.htm.

Toffler, Barbara Ley, with Jennifer Reingold. *Final Accounting: Ambition, Greed, and the Fall of Arthur Andersen.* New York: Broadway Books, 2003.

Turner, Lynn E. "The State of Financial Reporting Today: An Unfinished Chapter." Speech at the University of Southern California, May 31, 2001. www.sec.gov/news/speech/spch496.htm.

Vatter, William J. *Managerial Accounting.* New York: Prentice Hall, 1950.

Wallison, Peter J. "Give Us Disclosure, Not Audits." *Wall Street Journal,* June 2, 2003.

Watts, Ross L. "The Evolution of Economics-Based Empirical Research in Accounting." Speech at Baruch College, April 14, 1983. http:// newman.baruch.cuny.edu/digital/saxe/saxe_1982/watts_83.htm.

Watts, Ross L., and Jerold L. Zimmerman. *Positive Accounting Theory.* Englewood Cliffs, NJ: Prentice-Hall, 1986.

Weber, Joseph Peter. "Shareholder Wealth Effects of Pooling-of-Interests Accounting: Evidence from the SEC's Restriction on Share Repurchases Following Pooling Transactions." October 2000. http://ssrn.com/abstract=246370.

Wei, Lingling. "FASB Is Expected to Issue Rule on Expensing of Stock Options." *Wall Street Journal,* December 15, 2004.

Weil, Jonathon. "How Leases Play a Shadowy Role in Accounting." *Wall Street Journal,* September 22, 2004.

Welch, Jack, with John A. Byrne. *Jack: Straight from the Gut.* New York: Warner Books, 2003.

Wise, T. A. "The Auditors Have Arrived." *Fortune,* November 1960.

Wolk, Harry I., James L. Dodd, and Michael G. Tearney. *Accounting Theory: Conceptual Issues in a Political and Economic Environment.* 6th ed. Mason, OH: Thomson South-Western, 2003.

Wyatt, Arthur. *A Critical Study of Business Combinations.* New York: AICPA, 1963.

Wyatt, Arthur. "Efficient Market Theory: Its Impact on Accounting." *Journal of Accountancy* (February 1983).

Yee, Kenton K. "Interim Reporting Frequency and Financial Analysts Expenditures." *Journal of Business, Finance, and Accounting* 31 (2004).

Zeff, Stephen A. *The American Accounting Association: Its First 50 Years, 1916–1966.* Sarasota, FL: American Accounting Association, 1991.

Zeff, Stephen A. "The Work of the Special Committee on Research Program." *Accounting Historians Journal* (December 2001).

INDEX

235

ABOUT THE AUTHOR

Tom King grew up in Racine, Wisconsin, and studied liberal arts at Harvard College. He worked for three years on the New York audit staff of Arthur Andersen & Co., earned an MS in accounting from New York University, and obtained CPA and CMA certification. After receiving an MBA from Harvard Business School, he joined Progressive Insurance in Cleveland. He spent 10 years in marketing and general management before returning to accounting. Since then he has served as corporate controller, investment strategist, and treasurer. Married with three children, he lives in Chagrin Falls, Ohio.